[GRIZZ WRITES]

A Guide to First-Year Writing at Oakland University

Edited by

LORI OSTERGAARD and D. R. HAMMONTREE

Associate Editors

**Matthew Burkett | Colleen Doyle | John Freeman
Amanda Laudig | Cathy Rorai**

FOUNTAINHEAD
PRESS

Our green initiatives include:

Electronic Products
We deliver products in non-paper form whenever possible. This includes pdf downloadables, flash drives, & CDs.

Electronic Samples
We use Xample, a new electronic sampling system. Instructor samples are sent via a personalized web page that links to pdf downloads.

FSC Certified Printers
All of our printers are certified by the Forest Service Council which promotes environmentally and socially responsible management of the world's forests. This program allows consumer groups, individual consumers, and businesses to work together hand-in-hand to promote responsible use of the world's forests as a renewable and sustainable resource.

Recycled Paper
Most of our products are printed on a minimum of 30% post-consumer waste recycled paper.

Support of Green Causes
When we do print, we donate a portion of our revenue to green causes. Listed below are a few of the organizations that have received donations from Fountainhead Press. We welcome your feedback and suggestions for contributions, as we are always searching for worthy initiatives.

Rainforest 2 Reef

Environmental Working Group

Books may be purchased for educational purposes.

For information, please call or write:

1-800-586-0330
Fountainhead Press
Southlake, TX 76092

Web Site: www.fountainheadpress.com
E-mail: customerservice@fountainheadpress.com

Fifth Edition

ISBN: 978-1-68036-285-5

Printed in the United States of America

TABLE OF CONTENTS

INTRODUCTION: Welcome to the Conversation vii

Part 1: The First-Year Writing Program at OU By Lori Ostergaard

What to Expect in Your Writing Classes. 1

See What You Have to Say: The Writing Process. 3

How Rhetoric Can Help Writers Reach and Influence Readers. 5

Avoiding Plagiarism Through Methodical Research Practices 9

Conducting Primary Research: Some Ethical Considerations 15

Why We Don't Teach School Grammar in this University
Writing Program 19

Part 2: Practices and Processes in First-Year Writing

CHAPTER 7: GENERAL EDUCATION, TRANSFER OF LEARNING, AND
WHY YOU TAKE COURSES OUTSIDE OF YOUR MAJOR (And How
to Get the Most Out of Them) *By Dana Lynn Driscoll*. 25

CHAPTER 8: ENTERING THE CONVERSATION: The Link between
the Academic Essay and Real Life *By Colleen Doyle*. 35

CHAPTER 9: CRITICAL READING AND THINKING: A How-To-Do-It
Guide to Savvy Reading *By Alice Horning*. 45

CHAPTER 10: IF YOU COULD ASK ANY QUESTION: Introducing
Open Inquiry-Based, Student-Centered Writing Projects
By Ben Bennett-Carpenter 57

CHAPTER 11: INTERVIEWING TECHNIQUES: What to Do Before, During, and After *By Marilyn Borner and Jenna Katz* 67

CHAPTER 12: VISUAL RHETORIC: Reading the World Around You *By Jill McKay Chrobak* 77

CHAPTER 13: SOURCES AS PERSPECTIVES: A Guide to Engaging and Critical Secondary Research *By Christina Moore* 87

CHAPTER 14: SYNTHESIS: Fusing Sources to Create Something New *By Marilyn Borner* 101

CHAPTER 15: CONSTRUCTING A SOLID PIECE OF WRITING: Peer Review and Collaboration *By Lauren Rinke.* 109

CHAPTER 16: BEYOND THE COLLEGE ESSAY: Writing Activities and How They Affect Our Place in Communities *By Laura Gabrion and Christina Hall* 123

Part 3: Writing Excellence Award Winning Essays

Chapter 17: Rhetorical Analysis
THE VALEDICTION FORBIDDING UNANALYZED RHETORICAL AGENDAS *By Caitlin Keech* 135

Chapter 18: Research Essay (2015 Winner)
PRISON REHABILITATION AND ITS EFFECTS *By Elizabeth Kellogg* 141

Chapter 19: Research Essay (2016 Winner)
GENETIC MODIFICATION OF CROPS: A Necessity? *By Anthony Polito* 151

Chapter 20: Reflective Essay
THE ACTUAL LAST, FINAL REFLECTION: Composing a Research Paper *By Emily Stamper* 165

Part 4: Academic Style Guides

CHAPTER 21: MLA Style Guide 171

CHAPTER 22: APA Style Guide 179

CHAPTER 23: Sample Student Paper in APA Format 187

ABOUT THE CHAPTER AUTHORS 193

ABOUT THE STUDENT AUTHORS 197

APPENDICES

Appendix A: First-Year Writing Class Descriptions 199

Appendix B: University and Department Policies 205

Appendix C: Online Course Work Expectations 211

Appendix D: Glossary of Terms Used in First-Year Writing 215

Appendix E: Student Support and Resources 223

Appendix F: Events and Activities 227

Appendix G: Earn a Writing and Rhetoric Major or Minor 229

INTRODUCTION:
Welcome to the Conversation

"Imagine that you enter a parlor. You come late. When you arrive, others have long preceded you, and they are engaged in a heated discussion, a discussion too heated for them to pause and tell you exactly what it is about. In fact, the discussion had already begun long before any of them got there, so that no one present is qualified to retrace for you all the steps that had gone before. You listen for a while, until you decide that you have caught the tenor of the argument; then you put in your oar."

— Kenneth Burke

Over the next four years you will learn to join the academic conversations taking place all over our campus, and this book will serve as your first guide through the process that Burke (1973) describes above. The academic conversations you will engage in as a student here will cover complex and sophisticated fields like biology, psychology, engineering, nursing, education, rhetoric, and philosophy, to name just a few. These conversations have been going on for decades, centuries, and millennia, but with the help of this guide and with the help of your first-year writing classes and your writing-intensive classes at Oakland University, you will learn to recognize and follow the unspoken rules of these conversations, discover where your knowledge fits into the "tenor of the argument" (Burke, 1973, p.110), and learn to participate confidently and rhetorically in the important conversational work going on all around us.

The writing program at OU is guided by research, theory, and best practices in the field of composition-rhetoric, and we've received national recognition for our work with first-year students. In fall 2012, our first-year writing program was awarded a Conference on College Composition and Communication Writing Program Certificate of Excellence. This award is given to only a handful of writing programs every year, and it is a testament to our exceptional faculty and innovative first-year writing curriculum.

In your first-year writing classes, you will be asked to interact with the world as a writer, as a person who observes, reflects, researches, seeks feedback, and composes texts designed to do work in the world. Your first-year writing instructors will introduce you to key steps in the writing process; teach you how to analyze rhetorical situations effectively; provide you with practice writing to a wide range of audiences; introduce you to the skills and knowledges necessary to compose everything from traditional print texts to new media compositions, websites, wikis, videos, and podcasts; instruct you in both primary and secondary research methods; teach you how to critically read and write a variety of texts; and lead you to consider your ethical responsibilities as a researcher.

Because our first-year writing faculty are expert writers themselves, they will provide you with valuable feedback on your writing throughout the semester. And because our faculty value collaboration and peer review, you will also gain important skills working with classmates to complete projects and offering feedback on your peers' papers and course projects. The feedback you receive in your first-year writing classes will lead you to reconsider and revise your texts. Offering and receiving constructive feedback will also help you to identify both your strengths and your weaknesses as a writer.

This book, like many of the projects you will compose in your first-year writing classes, is the work of many hands. The Chair of the Department of Writing and Rhetoric, Lori Ostergaard, wrote the chapters in Part One that detail various aspects of this writing program's approach to teaching writing. She was also responsible for compiling and editing this work, but she received feedback and editing support from her co-editor, D.R. Hammontree, and from associate editors Matthew Burkett, Colleen Doyle, John Freeman, Amanda Laudig, and Cathy Rorai. Additional support with the MLA and APA style guides was provided by Elizabeth Allan. Individual faculty members have also contributed to this text in chapters examining general education, academic conversations, open-inquiry research, critical reading strategies, the use of secondary research, synthesis, peer review, visual rhetoric, and writing beyond the classroom. Finally, students in our first-year writing program have contributed their Writing Excellence Award winning essays to this guide. Maybe one day your work will appear in this guide as well, as a model for other first-year students to aspire to and emulate.

This guide will lead you through all of the first-year writing classes you are required to take here at OU, so be prepared to use this book in your WRT 102, Basic Writing class; in WRT 150, Composition I; and in WRT 160, Composition II. In addition to chapters detailing various elements of our writing classes, this book contains important information about our course policies and classroom procedures. At the back of the guide we have also provided you with sections detailing both the Modern Language Association (MLA) and the American Psychological Association (APA) styles that you will use to document your secondary research in WRT 150, WRT 160, and beyond.

The First-Year Writing Program receives a small commission from the sale of this guide, which we direct back into the writing program here at OU. This means that some of the money you paid for this guide may go towards funding student activities sponsored by the First-Year Writing Program, including our Writing Marathons and Writing Excellence Awards. These proceeds may also be used for professional development training for our writing faculty, allowing your instructor to attend professional conferences and workshops to improve their teaching. Finally, funds from the sale of the guide may be re-directed into improving this guide as a resource for our first-year writing students.

We hope you will find this a handy and helpful resource as you navigate your way through the first-year writing program here at Oakland University.

Reference

Burke, K. (1973). *The Philosophy of Literary Form: Studies in Symbolic Action.* (3rd ed.). Berkeley: University of California Press, 110-11.

Part 1:
The First-Year Writing Program at Oakland University

[1]

WHAT TO EXPECT IN YOUR WRITING CLASSES

> *"The skill of writing is to create a context in which other people can think."*
>
> – Edwin Schlossberg

The quote above encapsulates just one part of the Department of Writing and Rhetoric's philosophy about writing. We believe that writing creates a space in which writers and readers may think, learn, and grow.

Writing in college entails much more than just a display of knowledge or a performance of skill: college writing is about extending, adapting, applying, testing, researching, or challenging knowledge. In the Department of Writing and Rhetoric, our faculty support this approach to college writing by acclimating you to Oakland University's community of writers, researchers, and thinkers; familiarizing you with the writing process; teaching you how to conduct some primary and secondary research; and introducing you to some important rhetorical strategies and approaches that will serve your writing in college and beyond.

Your writing instructor will assign a variety of projects and papers designed to teach you to think critically about the audiences you are writing to, apply effective rhetorical strategies, employ primary and secondary research, and address both academic and popular audiences with your written, visual, audio, and video compositions.

The sections that follow outline five key issues related to academic writing: writing processes, rhetoric, fair use of sources (including source documentation and avoiding plagiarism), ethical primary research practices, and the secondary role of small-scale issues (including grammar instruction, mechanics, diction, etc.). While these five issues are treated at length in this book, you should know that in addition to process, rhetoric, and ethical research practices, the writing faculty at OU value the following:

- Group work

- Peer review

- Revision

- Self-evaluation and self-reflective practices

- Primary and secondary research methods

- Audience analyses

- New media and multimodal composition

- Community engagement and community research

- Challenging assignments that require critical thinking, creativity, collaboration, and resourcefulness

- Students' sustained efforts at improving their writing

- Sustained, careful, and critical reading of a variety of texts

- Engaged and active classroom environments

Reference

Schlossberg, E. "For My Father." In John Brockman (Ed.), *About Bateson: Essays on Gregory Bateson*. (pp. 145-167). New York, NY: Dutton.

[2]

SEE WHAT YOU HAVE TO SAY:
The Writing Process

> *"How can I tell what I think till I see what I say?"*
>
> – E.M. Forster

Your instructor will engage your class in a process approach to writing that will involve brainstorming and prewriting strategies, drafting, peer reviewing, and revising your papers multiple times. By the time you leave your WRT classes, your written work will have been read and responded to by both classmates and your instructor multiple times throughout the semester, which will give you a better sense of both your strengths and your weaknesses as a writer. Be prepared to build on your strengths and work on your weaknesses during your subsequent writing and writing-intensive classes here at OU.

In our WRT classes you will find that one of the best ways to guarantee your success in writing papers in our classes and in classes across campus is to think about, draft, and research your papers early. Our research indicates that students who engage in **prewriting** activities early are less likely to plagiarize their written assignments and are more likely to earn high grades on their written work than students who do not engage in prewriting early in the process.

Your writing will also improve throughout the semester as you engage in **peer reviews** of your work and as you receive feedback from your instructor. Peer reviews play a central role in the lives of your professors in WRT and across the university. University faculty constantly engage in a process of peer review of their written work with colleagues, journal reviewers, editors, and publishers. Your professors use the peer reviews they receive to improve and, eventually, publish their research. You will engage in peer reviews regularly in your WRT classes as well, and you will discover that constructive peer review is critical for your success in college.

Our writing classes have been designed intentionally to require that you revisit, rework, and sometimes completely revise your written work multiple times throughout the semester. Professional writers view revision as an opportunity to improve, re-see, and fine tune their work, so when your writing instructor asks your class to revise a paper, you should take full advantage of this opportunity to revisit and strengthen your work. You should also view the **revision** that we require in your WRT classes as a kind of invisible requirement in all of the classes you take at OU. Any time you are assigned a paper for a class, make certain you have scheduled a reasonable amount of time in your research and writing process to get feedback from a friend, family member, faculty member, or consultant in the Writing Center and to revise your work according to that feedback.

In your WRT classes, you will learn to move between the various stages of the writing process—brainstorming, freewriting, mapping, sketching, outlining, drafting, peer reviewing, and revising—but keep in mind that the order of these stages is never fixed. Many writers find that after their written work has been reviewed and commented on, they need to return to the brainstorm or freewrite stage to discover ways to solve the problems or address the questions their readers have identified in their texts. Some writers may find that they spend too much time revising their work and too little time developing new ideas through freewriting; others may find that they need to learn to devote more time to mapping, sketching, and organizing their work, while still others may not spend enough time revising their work to better address their readers. You will leave your WRT class with a better understanding of your own writing process and with some effective strategies for improving your work at each stage in that process.

Reference

Forster, E.M. (1976). *Aspects of the novel.* New York: Penguin.

[3]

HOW RHETORIC CAN HELP WRITERS REACH AND INFLUENCE READERS

"[S]he who does not study rhetoric will be a victim of it."

– Found on a Greek wall, 6th Century B.C

Throughout your life both in and outside of college, you will be required to direct your writing to very specific audiences. Whether those audiences are colleagues at work, potential clients, employers, members of government, people in your local community, college professors, friends, or family, your writing must speak to those audiences.

In your WRT classes, we prepare you for this challenge by teaching you how to analyze your intended audience, identify your purpose, use rhetorical appeals effectively, and address specific rhetorical contexts for your work. We cannot teach you how to write every kind of document you will ever be required to write—letter, resume, proposal, memo, report, analysis, article, editorial, position statement, evaluation, review, etc—and we cannot teach you how to write for every possible audience you will encounter in your life, but we can teach you how to ask the right questions each time you compose for a new audience and a new rhetorical situation.

Your instructor will introduce you to considerations of audience, purpose, and rhetorical situation throughout the semester, asking you to keep each of these considerations in mind as you compose your work. Writers must always consider their audience's prior knowledge, values, expectations, biases, etc, before they begin to write for that audience. Writers must also have a clear idea of the purpose for their writing—to inform, persuade, or entertain. And they must be aware of the rhetorical context for their work, of the situations and circumstances surrounding their topic, of the ways their work will be received, of the rhetorical strategies that will work best with their particular audience, and of the consequences of their joining a particular conversation.

Because you will be writing for specific audiences in your WRT classes and beyond, it might be helpful for you to learn a few basic rhetorical terms that explain how effective speakers and writers work to address and influence their audiences.

One of the most important things you will need to keep in mind is how you come across to your audience. You will want to consider, in other words, your **ethos**. *Ethos* is a Greek term that translates, roughly, as the writer's authority, credibility, or character. Your audience will be more willing to listen to you, will be more likely to be moved or persuaded by your text, if you come across as a "good [person] speaking well" (Quintilian 12.1.1). In other words, your audience will want to know that you are familiar with the topic, you have done your research, and you have good reasons for speaking on your topic. Some audiences, particularly academic ones, will want to know that you are a member of their academic community, that you speak their academic language, are familiar with the same research and scholarship that they are familiar with, and know how to properly cite that research in your work. But every audience will need to know that you have their best interests in mind and that you know what you are talking about. As a writer, you will want to develop subtle and sophisticated strategies for illustrating your *ethos* to your audience, and your WRT instructor can help you learn to do this effectively.

In addition to determining what your ethos is with a particular audience, and how you might need to persuade that audience of your authority to speak on a subject, you will want to consider how to move your audience's emotions with your text. The Greek term for the practice of using words (images, sounds, etc) to sway an audience's emotions is **pathos**. One type of effective pathetic (emotional) appeal is a narrative that can take an abstract issue like gang violence and put a human face on that issue. The story of a little girl whose beloved older brother was killed by a stray bullet will have a greater emotional appeal than a report detailing the number of fatalities caused by gang violence every year. Other ways to construct emotional appeals in your writing are to use metaphors, vivid descriptions, and the repetition of powerful words of phrases.

While pathetic appeals work with a variety of audiences outside of the university, they are not typically as welcomed within the academy as appeals to reason or **logos**. We get the word "logic" from the Greek word *logos*, and it signifies a claim that is based in fact or reason (rather than emotion or character). Statistics and survey data can be used as appeals to logic, as can claims supported by sound reasoning. As a writer, you will need to know how much information your audience will need to know, what type of information your audience respects (personal accounts or statistics, observations or experiments, reasoned claims or quotes from respected sources), and how much information they already know so that you do not insult their intelligence. You will also need to know how to construct logical claims that you can support with expert voices, evidence, and examples. While the story of the little girl above may appeal to readers outside of the university, most of your university professors will respond better to a claim that is supported using the report detailing the number of fatalities instead.

Finally, you will be asked to think about the context for your work in your WRT classes and beyond. **Kairos** is the term we use to mean "the opportune moment," the perfect moment for speaking (or acting) on a particular issue. When rhetorician and author Karen Schriver (1989) observed that "whether 'knowledge' gets noticed at all is partly a matter of whether the community is ready and willing to listen," she was referring to the *kairotic* moment (p.

273). An understanding of *kairos* will help you to decide if your audience is ready to listen to your topic or if you need to construct the *kairotic* moment to help your audience appreciate the urgency or relevance of your topic. For example, if you were to write about gang violence, your audience would be more likely to listen to you if you opened your essay by discussing some current event or recent finding associated with this issue.

As you work your way through your WRT courses, you will learn to recognize when the authors you read (both in your assigned texts and in the texts composed by your classmates) use *ethos, pathos, logos,* and *kairos* effectively to address their audiences. Each of these appeals will work to a different extent on different readers, and you will need to learn how different readers tend to respond to each appeal.

The **format, forum, and medium** of your work will also need to meet the expectations of your readers. To reach your intended audience and achieve your intended purposes with your compositions, you may be called upon to write an essay, a report, a whitepaper, a memo, a speech or presentation, a letter, an article, a website, a wiki, an audio essay, a video, etc. With each new challenge you encounter in your WRT classes and beyond, ask yourself "who is my audience," "what is my purpose," "what persuasive appeals will work with this audience to achieve my purpose," and "where does my work fit into the conversation?"

For a short primer on rhetoric, visit Professor Jim Nugent's website: http://tech-rhet.net/resources/rhetoric/

References

Quintilian, M. F. (1920). *Institutio Oratoria.* (H.E. Butler, Trans). Cambridge, MA: Harvard University Press. (Original work published 95 CE).

Schriver, K. A. (1989). Theory building in rhetoric and composition: The role of empirical scholarship. *Rhetoric Review, 7,* 272-288. doi: 10.1080/07350198909388861

[4]

AVOIDING PLAGIARISM THROUGH METHODICAL RESEARCH PRACTICES

One of the most important lessons you will learn in your writing classes relates to preventing plagiarism in your research and compositions for classes across the university. Frequently plagiarism gets condensed to a set of rules, but the real issue with plagiarism is that when writers and researchers appropriate other people's work, they do not create any new knowledge, and they risk damaging their ethos with their audience. Creating new knowledge is the real work of the university: OU students, faculty, researchers, and administrators dedicate their time here to the construction of knowledge. So when your class discusses this important issue, remember that one of the reasons plagiarism is treated so seriously is that your professors expect you to contribute to the knowledge-building work of this institution.

Your WRT instructor will introduce and explain the university's academic integrity regulations, leading you through the composition of an academic research project, but there are a number of strategies you can employ to prevent plagiarism in your work as well.

Begin drafting all of your papers early. Our research indicates that students who engage in pre-writing for their papers are less likely to accidentally plagiarize their sources. The minute a paper is assigned to you in any class at the university, you should begin pre-writing on your topic to determine what it is you already know, think, feel, or intuit about that topic. Write down as many ideas and as many research questions as you possibly can. Write a tentative outline for your paper before you begin researching, but keep in mind that your outline, and your ideas and research questions, may change dramatically as you continue to research and write about your topic.

Be a careful researcher. Keep a research notebook on your computer's desktop and open that notebook whenever you find a new source. Before you copy a single quote from that source, copy/paste the citation information for that source into your notebook. Then copy/paste the quotes you want to use (making a note of the page number or paragraph where each quote can be found) into your notebook. You might want to compose your paraphrases of each quote in this notebook as well, including the original quote above your paraphrase for future reference. Finally, when you do insert a quote or paraphrase into your paper, make sure you include the citation with the author's name and page number. You can edit these citations later to bring them in line with either MLA or APA style, but you will want to include some kind of reference to your source the minute you use that source material in your paper. Once your quote or paraphrase has been entered into your paper and cited, highlight it or change the font color. This way, the information that is not your own will stand out as you begin to revise your work over the next couple of months, and you will be able to distinguish between your words and the quotes or paraphrases of another author. When it is time to turn in your paper, you can remove the highlights or change all of the fonts back to black.

Paraphrase by imagining that you are explaining what each difficult passage says to a friend. Paraphrasing can count as plagiarism if all you do is use a thesaurus to replace each word in the original quote with a synonym. Instead, you need to put each passage you paraphrase into your own words, altering both the words and the order of the original passage without altering the author's intent or meaning. The easiest way to do this is to read the passage you want to paraphrase through a couple of times, then push that passage out of sight and pretend you are explaining what that passage says to a friend. If you get really stumped paraphrasing a difficult passage, imagine that you are a character from a movie or television show and paraphrase the difficult passage in that character's voice (Tony Soprano, Donald Trump, Lady Gaga). You will need to put the character's paraphrase into an academic voice when you're finished, but this silly exercise might help you find a new way to paraphrase the passage. When you have finished paraphrasing a passage from another text, review your paraphrase to confirm that it accurately reflects the same idea included in the original passage, but that it does not sound at all like the other author's original phrasing.

Understand citation practices. Your papers will be written in MLA style in your WRT 102 and WRT 150 classes and in APA style in your WRT 160 class. You may already be familiar with MLA style from your high school English classes, but only about 3% of OU students will actually use MLA style in their upper-level classes. Most OU students will encounter APA style in their upper-level business, health sciences, nursing, psychology, education, and communications courses , so WRT 160 provides you with an opportunity to transition from the citation style you are accustomed to into the one you will use the most during your four years here.

No matter what style you use, though, you must know how and when to cite a source. Any time you use another writer's ideas, research, questions, quotes, summaries, charts, images, abstracts, etc, you must cite that author. Any time you paraphrase another author, you must cite that author. And your citation must follow immediately after each quote or paraphrase you use. This means that you cannot apply a "blanket" citation for an entire paragraph by putting the citation at the end of the paragraph; instead, you will need to cite each and every instance when you use someone else's work. And when in doubt, cite it.

Employ primary research. Our research shows that students who use some primary sources (interviews, surveys, questionnaires, participant-observation) in their research papers are less likely to accidentally plagiarize their secondary sources than students who do not incorporate any primary research into their work. If your instructor permits the inclusion of primary research, then it might be a good idea to gather some of your own primary information for your paper. Since you may not be familiar with the methods and ethics of this kind of research, plan to work closely with your WRT instructor to develop your survey or interview questions, to determine how best to protect your sources, and to discover how to incorporate this information into your paper.

Understand common knowledge. "Common knowledge" is the term applied to any information that is held in common by a particular community and, thus, does not require source citation. For example, many of us would consider the claim that "Christopher Columbus discovered America" to be common knowledge, and we would not expect anyone to cite a source for that information. But common knowledge is such a complicated issue that even most academics cannot agree on a definition of the term, and common knowledge varies sometimes radically according to your audience. For example, in the claim about Columbus above, a writer might not get into trouble saying, without citing, that statement if s/he were writing to readers of more popular or public texts. However, if the writer were to make that claim in a university history class where Columbus's "discovery" of a continent already inhabited by millions of people was in contention, that writer should probably cite the source for that claim. As a student, you will want to be especially careful about using (and not citing) common knowledge for this reason. If you aren't sure if something would be considered common knowledge by your readers, arrange to meet with your professor before your paper is due, asking that s/he tell you what information/claims in your paper may count as common knowledge, and what information should be cited. And when in doubt, cite it.

Conference with your professor. Our research suggests that students who meet with their professors outside of class to discuss their papers are less likely to plagiarize, so take advantage of your professors' office hours or make appointments to meet outside of class to ask that they read and comment on your work before you submit it for a grade. Notify your professor in advance that you will be stopping by during their office hours and that you will want them to read and discuss your paper with them during that time. Bring two clean copies of your paper with you so that both you and your professor can take notes during your paper conference, and before you leave the conference, restate what you think your professor has suggested you need to do to improve your work. If you are concerned about source citation and plagiarism in particular, ask your professor to be on the lookout for this as s/he reads your work. While a 20-minute meeting may be sufficient time to discuss a 3-5 page paper, you may need to meet several times with your professor to get feedback on a longer work.

Visit the Writing Center. The undergraduate writing consultants who work in the university's Writing Center, in Kresge Library, have been taught to help students with every aspect of the writing process, from prewriting to revising. While they will not copy-edit your papers for you, these expert consultants are adept at citing sources in a variety of academic styles, and they can provide you with a second set of eyes to spot faulty source citation or plagiarism in your papers.

The University's Procedures for Adjudicating Suspected Plagiarism

The university community believes that cheating on examinations, plagiarism, falsifying reports/records, and unauthorized collaboration, access, or modifying of computer programs are considered serious breaches of academic conduct (Oakland University).

One goal of the first-year writing program is to teach you how to avoid plagiarism in your academic and professional writing, and we are required to follow the university's procedures if we suspect a student has plagiarized any written work. If upon reviewing a student project, an instructor suspects that a student has plagiarized, the instructor will issue an incomplete on the assignment and forward the matter with a letter of explanation and supporting documentation to the Office of the Dean of Students. Penalties for plagiarism may include a failing grade in the course, academic probation, and suspension. Students who have been found to have plagiarized are also required to attend the Cite Right program, hosted by OU's Writing Center.

Once the matter has been resolved by the Academic Conduct Committee, the WRT faculty member will issue the appropriate grade on the assignment. If an Incomplete has been issued for the final course grade, the instructor will complete a change of grade form as appropriate.

The penalties for plagiarism are serious, but if you work closely with your course instructor to make certain you understand how to avoid plagiarism, follow the suggestions above, and begin your research and composition processes early, you should not have any problems with plagiarism during your time here. Additional information about OU's Academic Conduct Regulations is available in the OU Student Handbook (http://catalog.oakland.edu/content.php?catoid=14&navoid=700).

Reference

Oakland University. Academic conduct regulations. Retrieved May 21, 2012, from: http://www.oakland.edu/?id=1610&sid=75

[5]

CONDUCTING PRIMARY RESEARCH:
Some Ethical Considerations

You may be asked to conduct some primary research in your first-year writing classes. While you are probably familiar with secondary research, where you cite the research findings and scholarly interpretations of others, you may not have encountered primary research methods before now. Briefly, primary research is the research you conduct yourself through observations, surveys, interviews, questionnaires, or experiments.

In your first-year writing classes, you probably won't be asked to conduct lab experiments, but you may be asked to conduct interviews or surveys to supplement your secondary research of a topic. For example, if you were to research the mythical "Freshman Fifteen," you would want to gather secondary research from nutrition researchers and, possibly, social scientists who have investigated this phenomenon. But you might also want to gather your own research by surveying first-year students at OU to find out if they've gained or lost weight in college, to discover their eating habits, and to find out what kinds of exercise they do. Your research report on this topic would include both what the "experts" say and what you discovered in your own research.

While conducting your own research into a topic can be both fun and informative, and this kind of research can contribute greatly to your ethos as an academic writer, there are a number of important ethical issues that you will need to consider before you undertake any primary research.

Inform Your Research Participants. As an ethical researcher, you will want to make sure that the people you observe, survey, or interview understand why you are engaging with them. You should always reveal the nature and scope of your research project up front by informing participants that you are conducting this research for a class and explaining what your topic and focus are. If you think you might eventually publish (in print or on the web) or present this research, you should inform your research participants of this so that they understand that your class project might have a life beyond the classroom. One effective way of ensuring that your participants agree to be a part of your research is to ask them to sign an informed consent form explaining your research and their role in it.

Protect Your Research Participants. As an ethical researcher, you will want to make certain that your research will not, at any time or in any way, endanger your research participants. While you would obviously not ask participants to engage in illegal or dangerous activities for the purpose of your research, you should also consider other ways that your work might potentially endanger participants by damaging their reputations now or in the future. The people you interview or survey for your research may wish to remain anonymous in your work, so offer them the option of choosing a pseudonym. And always be respectful and understanding when a potential research participant asks not to be a part of your research.

Be Aware of How You Use Your Participants' Photographed or Videotaped Images. Your research projects may involve photos or videotapes of your research participants, and while we live in an age of instantaneous video uploads to the web, as an ethical researcher, you will still want to make certain that your research subjects are aware of where their image may eventually appear. If you plan to show your research video or photographs to an audience beyond your first-year writing class or if you plan to upload it to the web, make certain that your research participants are aware of your plans and agree to your presentation or publication of their photographed or videotaped image. One easy way to make certain research participants understand and agree to all of the items listed above is by getting their informed consent (in writing) for participation in your research.

Get Informed Consent from Your Research Participants. If you engage in primary research for your class projects, you will probably want to develop an "Informed Consent" form that tells participants about your research project, explains their role in that project, informs them of where you might publish or present your research, and states some policy for protecting their identities. An informed consent form, one that both you and your research participants sign, can help you to do all of these things quickly and efficiently. Your course instructor can help you draft an informed consent form for your primary research or provide your class with a model form to use. Just make certain that all of your research participants are above the age of 18 so that they can legally give their informed consent. If you are researching children or young adults below the age of 18, make certain you get their parents' informed consent.

Incorporate Your Primary Research into Your Project. When you compose your research project, you will want to distinguish between the research you conducted yourself and the secondary sources you collected. For this reason, your research should probably be included in a separate section of your paper, unless your course instructor suggests otherwise. Your own research should probably not be included in the Review of Lit section, but you may want to mention any primary research you conducted in your paper's abstract so that readers will know to expect some primary data in addition to secondary research.

Explain Your Research Methods to Your Readers. Finally, you should be prepared to describe the methods you used to gather your research (how/where you found your participants, how many participants you used in your research, who those participants were, what kinds of questions you asked them, etc). Many of the published authors you will read in your first-year writing classes will discuss their research methods, so you may want to pay attention to and model how these published researchers compose their own methods sections. By including a discussion of your primary research methods in your project, you'll show readers that you are a careful and ethical researcher, someone whose data and analysis they can trust.

[6]

WHY WE DON'T TEACH SCHOOL GRAMMAR IN THIS UNIVERSITY WRITING PROGRAM

You may be surprised to learn that you will not be engaging in lessons, work-shops, or quizzes that will instruct you in the proper use of Standardized American English grammar in your Writing and Rhetoric classes at OU. There are two very simple reasons why we don't provide direct instruction in gram-mar in our writing classes. The first reason is that all of the available research tells us that direct instruction in grammar does nothing to improve writing. The second reason is that, as with "beauty," grammatical correctness is often in the eye of the beholder. What one audience considers "correct," another may consider "incorrect." In other words, when we talk about grammar in our first-year writing classes, we talk about it in the context of your work, your audience, and your purpose as a writer. Grammar is rhetorical: it is tied to specific writing situations, purposes, and reader expectations.

What the Research Tells Us

OU's first-year writing classes do not provide direct instruction in grammar because research in the field of composition demonstrates that this kind of instruction does not help students to develop their writing and rhetorical skills or their proficiency as effective communicators. In fact, the available research clearly demonstrates that writing class time spent discussing grammar may actually be a bad thing since this work takes away from time that is better spent instructing in writing and rhetoric. Indeed, in his metastudy (i.e. survey of all previous research) of the grammar debate in composition, Hartwell (1985) summarized 75 years worth of empirical data that clearly illustrates that "there is no 'relationship between a knowledge of technical grammar and the ability to use English and interpret language'" (p. 126). Hartwell cites another metastudy from 1959 that revealed that "in all these studies, carried out in places and at times far removed from each other, often by highly experienced and disinterested investigators, the results have been consistently negative so far as the value of grammar in the improvement of language expression is concerned" (DeBoer as cited in Hartwell, 1985, p. 126). Likewise, Hillocks's (1987) "Synthesis of Research on Teaching Writing" reveals that "the study of traditional school grammar (i.e., the definition of parts of speech, the parsing of sentences, etc.) has no effect on raising the quality of student writing. . . . Moreover, a heavy emphasis on mechanics and usage (e.g., marking every error) results in significant losses in overall [writing] quality" (p. 74). Direct instruction in grammar, in other words, will not result in any improvements to your writing skills.

The reason grammar instruction does not improve writing skill is best explained through an analogy. If you recall when you learned to drive, before they let you get behind the wheel of the family car, your parents probably did not first require that you learn to take the car engine apart, memorize all of the parts of that engine, and explain how they all worked together. In other words, before they would let you drive, your parents didn't expect you to understand how cars accelerate; you needed only to know that pressing on the gas pedal would make the car go. None of us needs to know how a fuel injector works before we can become truly adept drivers.

The same basic principle applies for native speakers of English. No one expected you to know what a prepositional phrase, an indirect object, or a restrictive clause was before you began communicating in English as a toddler. Language and communication are hard-wired into the DNA of all humans, and even at a young age, children begin to internalize and apply some very complex grammatical rules without ever having to be introduced to those rules in the classroom.

You've already used language effectively in a number of challenging rhetorical situations over the last seventeen years of your life. You don't need to be able to name all of the parts of speech and explain how they all work together to communicate effectively in speech or in writing. Just as you don't need to be able to identify a carburetor or explain how it works before you can drive a car, you don't need to know what a relative pronoun is or how it works before you can communicate effectively. Studying grammar may make you a better grammarian, but even university faculty who research language use—linguists—will tell you that this knowledge has no impact on how well you communicate in writing or in speaking to others.

What you will learn in your first-year writing classes is strategies and approaches for writing to new, and increasingly demanding, audiences: college faculty, community leaders, educated peers, employers, and the general public. Our classes will help you figure out the most effective ways to address those audiences by first analyzing what those audiences value, what they expect of writers, and what will persuade them. These are the questions that all writers must be able to answer about the people they write to, and these challenging questions have very little to do with your ability to identify a subordinate clause or a dangling modifier.

Understanding Grammar in Context

Even if the research did not demonstrate the inefficacy of grammatical instruction in the writing classroom, it would still be a waste of class time to teach you Standardized American English grammar and mechanics. This is because different audiences have different ideas about what constitutes "correct" grammar. For example, if you are writing to a college English professor who uses MLA style, that professor will expect you to add an additional comma before "and" in a list of three or more things: cats, dogs, and fish. If you write the same list in an essay for a college journalism professor who uses AP style, that professor will expect you to eliminate that additional comma before "and": cats, dogs and fish. What is correct in one context, with one audience, may be incorrect, an error, in another context and with another audience.

As a writer, you will make both large and small rhetorical decisions as you write, choosing the most rhetorically appropriate and powerful ways to communicate your ideas to an audience. Your writing style, grammar, and (as the example above suggests) even your punctuation choices may well depend on who your audience is and what you hope to accomplish with your writing. Here are some examples of the kinds of grammar questions you might have to consider as you write:

- Are abbreviations OK to use with your readers?

- What about contractions?

- How formal should your style be?

- Will your readers be offended if you split an infinitive? Will they think you're being pretentious if you don't split an infinitive?

- Will your readers expect you to use titles (Mr., Ms., Dr.)? Will they want you to use first and last names, first initials and last names, or last names only in your texts?

- Are your readers likely to take issue with you if you ask "can I" rather than "may I"?

- Do your readers use non-gendered pronouns, even when doing so might be considered grammatically incorrect in some other circles: "every*one* should bring *their* book to class"?

College writers understand that some grammar rules (some of the ones you have learned since infancy) are dependable no matter who your audience is, but many other so-called *rules* are context-dependent. Thinking rhetorically about grammar will provide you with the guidance you need to make good choices as a writer.

Finally, while considerations of grammar and style are important "micro" aspects of writing, they are also the aspects you should worry about last in your writing process. Needlessly worrying about word choice or comma placement early in the writing process may prevent you from dealing effectively with the "macro" aspects of writing, like content and support, rhetorical appeals, and organization.

References

Hartwell, P. (1985). Grammar, grammars, and the teaching of grammar. *College English,* 47, 105-127. doi: 10.2307/376562

Hillocks, G. (1987). Synthesis of research on teaching writing. *Educational Leadership,* 44, 71-82. Retrieved from *www.ascd.org/ASCD/pdf/ journals/ed_lead/el_198705_hillocks.pdf*

Part 2:
Practices and Processes in First-Year Writing

[7]

GENERAL EDUCATION, TRANSFER OF LEARNING, AND WHY YOU TAKE COURSES OUTSIDE OF YOUR MAJOR

(And How to Get the Most Out of Them)

Dana Lynn Driscoll

Why do I have to take so many general education classes? Will this writing class really help me? Why do these classes seem to have nothing to do with my major? These are questions that many students ask as they begin their coursework at Oakland University. This chapter answers some of these questions, first by describing some conversations I've had with student writers concerning writing, transfer of learning, and general education. The next section provides a bit of background into the history, purpose, and decision-making surrounding general education courses, including your general education writing foundations course (WRT 160 and its prerequisites, WRT 102 and WRT 150). Then you will learn the answers to the "so what, who cares" questions through an examination of learning research that demonstrates that your general education courses actually matter. The final section provides some suggestions for how you can use these courses for your own future success in a wide variety of areas.

General Education and Writing Coursework: Students' Opinions

In the last six years, I've conducted almost 100 interviews with college writers and faculty trying to better understand how students learn to write, how faculty conceptualize and teach writing, and why students have such difficulty in transferring their learning; that is, identifying what is important and adapting that knowledge to new circumstances. Through these conversations with students, some interesting patterns have emerged concerning their beliefs about writing, as well as their views on courses within a general education curriculum, of which your writing courses, including WRT 160 are a part.

Aaron, a first-year graphic design student who had recently completed his writing courses, had a lot to say about his first year writing (FYW) class, "Its like, burn everything [from FYW]. . . . Once I'm done with writing I'm like, 'Ok I don't have to do any more writing. I don't care.'" While this view is extreme, it is one held, to some degree, by many of the other students interviewed for this study. Some students see writing (or other kinds of learning they do in general education courses) as disconnected from their future careers and therefore, not all that useful to them as students. Another student, Alice, a second-year student majoring in psychology, said this about her general education courses, "I hate them. I still hate them. Gen Eds can be fun but you know I'm not here for fun . . . but my time here would be so much shorter and so much cheaper if I didn't have to take Gen Eds. And for someone like me who came into college knowing what I wanted to do, I have always known what I wanted to do so for me it's just like extra fluff. It's just me throwing away money. . . . That was like a $1,000 that I just wasted."

Typically, half the students interviewed in this study fall into the belief systems above—not seeing writing and other general education courses they are taking as useful to their future careers or seeing them as a waste of time or money. If general education courses were such a waste, wouldn't the university have gotten rid of such courses long ago and only focused on your major? The truth is, these courses have a rich history and a specific purpose. This next section will describe why you have to take such courses and what their goals are for you as a student.

General Education and Writing Instruction: A Short History

Several hundred years ago, universities did not prepare students for particular kinds of careers nor did they teach profession-oriented subjects like nursing, engineering, psychology or business. All students who enrolled at the university took the same coursework designed to provide a broad set of educational experiences intended to create well-rounded individuals. This coursework included the classics, Latin and Greek, writing, history, and philosophy. The goal of university education, then, as Brody (1977) describes, was to educate you as a whole citizen, a person able to contribute to society in many different ways (professionally, civically, personally, educationally) and prepare you to adapt your knowledge to a wide set of circumstances. Upon leaving the university, you were expected to use your knowledge in a variety of ways to better society as well as your own interests. As Williams (1990) describes, this "whole person education" mission was, and continues to be, particularly true of publically-funded universities like Oakland whose missions include creating well-rounded, literate citizens and engaging in service to the public. Because the public helps fund your education, the idea is that your education should do more than just prepare you for a career, but rather give you a set of educational experiences to make you a good community member and citizen. This is why so many of our founding fathers, like Thomas Jefferson, supported a strong educational system in the first place; they believed it was critical for democracy to flourish.

In the 19th century with the rise of industralization, universities began to offer profession-oriented curriculums that would prepare students for working in more specialized fields. While this was occurring, universities began to attract a wider diversity of students, not all of whom were prepared for college-level writing and other university coursework. The end of the 19th century was also the first time that we saw first-year writing curriculum taught in university settings (Harris, 1997). These curricular and demographic shifts continued throughout the 20th century, when we had the GI-Bill in the 1950s and the "open admissions" movement of the 1970s which allowed more and more students to gain access to higher education. While these shifts in the student populations seeking higher education and the more professional and vocationally-based curriculums were happening, a rising tension occurred between the older general education curriculum and newer profession-focused curriculum (Benander & Lightner, 2005).

Today, universities resolve the tension by creating general education coursework that prepares you for college-level writing, gives you a basic understanding of Western and global issues, and exposes you to the various sciences, such as social sciences, humanities, and arts curricula. As the quotations mentioned earlier indicate, many of today's university students unfortunately do not realize the goals, purposes, or rich history of the general education courses they are being taught. But recent research has demonstrated that general education curriculum continues to be one of the most valuable aspects of a student's career.

Who makes the decisions about writing and other general education coursework?

Now that you understand some of the beliefs, history, and goals of general education curriculum, it's also important to understand how it works at Oakland. My interviews with students revealed most students have no idea of the curricular decision-making processes at universities, and understanding this information helped them better appreciate general education courses. At OU, university-wide general education decisions are made by the General Education Committee, made up of a rotating group of 12 faculty members and one undergraduate student (elected by the University Student Congress) as well as five non-voting campus administrators. This committee is responsible for evaluating potential general education courses, providing feedback on general education course assessments (that is, seeing how effective the courses are), and proposing changes to the curriculum. Your WRT 102, WRT 150, and WRT 160 courses are assessed and developed by a group of full and part-time faculty from within the department of Writing and Rhetoric. In other words, a great deal of thought, care, and a variety of perspectives goes into deciding what general education and writing curriculum is best for you as an OU student.

What skills do general education curricula teach?

In the 21st century, the university seeks to prepare you for specialized careers that are ever-changing while also teaching you a broad set of skills that can be adapted to diverse circumstances. These broad skills include literacy, rhetoric, information management, critical thinking, cultural knowledge, scientific literacy, and problem solving. One of the greatest challenges OU faculty face in educating students is the ever-changing nature of the 21st century workplace. According to the US Bureau of Labor Statistics (2012), data suggests that people change jobs, and sometimes even careers, anywhere between five and 11 times. Furthermore, today's workplaces are fast-paced, engage in rapid change, inter-culturally connected, and information-enriched. If your OU coursework only prepares you for the job you plan to do when you graduate, we have done you a substantial disservice because your knowledge will be quickly outdated as time passes. What we try to do with a general education curriculum is have you be a well-rounded critical thinker who is able to evaluate and adapt information, write effectively, and solve problems so that if you find yourself in new situations for which you weren't prepared, you are still able to learn and adapt your existing knowledge effectively. Beyond the workplace, the kinds of broad skills you gain in your general education classes may also help you make good decisions when it comes to being a member of our society.

Research also shows us that being an expert in any area, such as your field of study, actually requires you to have a broad knowledge base. General education is one of the keys to developing a large knowledge base, which is crucial for developing expertise on any one subject and being able to transfer knowledge from school settings to workplace settings (National Research Council, 1999).

Concerning your general education writing courses, the importance of these skills cannot be understated. The National Commission on Writing (2004) describes the results of a survey sent to 120 of the top corporations in the world, corporations that currently employ more than 8 million people. This survey revealed that writing is an essential skill for salaried employees. Over half of the responding companies report that they consider writing ability a critical criterion when hiring and promoting employees. Two-thirds of salaried employees in these companies are required to write a variety of workplace documents including reports, white papers, correspondence with employees and customers, and more.

Getting the Most out of General Education

Researchers have found students can greatly impact the success or failure of any learning experience, and that it is as much about what is taught as the mindset through which the material is approached (Driscoll and Wells, 2012). In other words, as a learner, you have to be responsible for recognizing the value in your coursework, seeking to adapt and use that coursework, and expanding your own view of what is "relevant" or "useful." The following suggestions, some of which come from the Framework for Success in Post-Secondary Writing (2011) and some from my own work (Driscoll, 2011), can help you get the most out of your general education courses:

- **Openness.** You should remain open to understanding that all knowledge has value even if that value is not immediately clear. Keep your mind open as you go through your coursework and recognize that there is much you don't yet know about your future. All knowledge has value.

- **Metacognition.** Metacognition asks you to take an active part in your own learning—monitor your learning processes, seek to understand how you learn best, learn from your mistakes and successes, and be aware of how you are growing as a learner.

- **Engagement.** Engagement refers to your ability to invest time and energy in your own learning. Realize that you are at a unique time in your life where you can dedicate yourself to learning and bettering yourself as an individual. Take advantage of this time, and learn to value it.

- **Building connections.** Seek to build connections between your current general education courses, your major coursework, your experiences with internships/co-ops/placements, and your personal life. These connections will help you with those important skills, like critical thinking and communication, which are necessary for the 21st century workplace.

- **Educating yourself about your future.** What skills really matter? What does a person in X career actually do on a daily basis? Seek out opportunities to learn about all aspects of your career.

Department of Writing and Rhetoric

Students who are able to embrace these qualities have a much better educational experience and are able to more successfully adapt and use what they learned in a wide variety of circumstances. By approaching all of your coursework with the right mindset, you can gain a great deal from your general education courses at Oakland University.

Questions for Discussion:

1. Why do you think tensions exist between teaching for specific skills vs. general knowledge at the university?

2. Do you think that changing information technology practices impact the need for general education?

3. Why do you think students have negative attitudes about general education courses?

4. What other benefits do you see in a curriculum that includes general education?

5. What is the purpose of general education at Oakland University?

6. Why is transfer of learning, or the ability to take or adapt knowledge from your courses to new circumstances, so important?

7. How might you use writing in your future career? In your future personal life?

8. For WRT 160 students: Take a look at your WRT 160 course syllabus and examine the general education language. What does this course seek to do? How have we met these goals thus far?

References

Bailyn, B. (1960). *Education in the forming of American society.* Chapel Hill, NC: U of North Carolina Press.

Benander, R., & Lightner, R. (2005). Promoting transfer of learning: Connecting general education courses. *The Journal of General Education, 54*(3), 199-208. doi: 10.1353/jge.2006.0001

Broudy, H.S. (1977). Types of knowledge and purposes in education. In R. C. Anderson, R. J. Spiro & W. E. Montague (Eds.), *Schooling and the Aquisition of Knowledge*. Hillsdale, NJ: Erlbaum.

Bureau of Labor Statistics (2012). Number of jobs held, labor market activity, and earnings growth among the youngest baby boomers: Results from a longitudinal survey. Washington, DC: U.S. Department of Labor. Retrieved from http://www.bls.gov/news.release/pdf/nlsoy.pdf

Council of Writing Program Administrators, National Council of Teachers of English, and National Writing Project (2011). *The framework for success in post-secondary writing*. Retrieved from http://wpacouncil.org/framework

Driscoll, D.L. (2011). Connected, disconnected, or uncertain: Student attitudes about future writing contexts and perceptions of transfer from first-year writing to the disciplines. Across the Disciplines, 8(2). Retrieved from http://wac.colostate.edu/atd/articles/driscoll2011/index.cfm.

Driscoll, D.L., & Wells, J. (2012). Beyond knowledge and skills: Writing transfer and the role of student dispositions. *Composition Forum, 26*. Retrieved from http://compositionforum.com/issue/26/beyond-knowledge-skills.php

Harris, J. (1997). *A teaching subject: Composition since 1966*. New York NY: Prentice Hall.

National Commission on Writing (2004). *Writing: A ticket to work....or a ticket out: A survey of business leaders*. College Board. Retrieved from http://www.writingcommission.org/prod_downloads/writingcom/writing-ticket-to-work.pdf

National Research Council (1999). *How people learn: Brain, mind, experience, and school*. Washington D.C: National Academy Press.

Oakland University (2011). *General education philosophy*. Retrieved from http://www2.oakland.edu/gened/philosophy.cfm

Presno, C. (1998). Assessing the value of general education programs: The addition of meaning-making to the e-value-ation process. *Education, 118*. Retrieved from http://www.projectinnovation.biz/education_2006.html

Williams, R.L. (1991). *The origins of federal support for higher education: George W. Atherton and the land-grant college movement*. University Park, PA: Pennsylvania State University Press.

[8]

ENTERING THE CONVERSATION:
The Link between the Academic Essay and Real Life

Colleen Doyle

Soon you'll be assigned your first college essay. You may wonder how this assignment will differ from high school, if this work will be just like high school or completely different, and if you'll be up for the challenges your first college essay entails. These are questions every first-year college student has asked him- or herself since there first were colleges to attend.

Academic research essays are the basis for generating knowledge in undergraduate education. This knowledge and research is what helps run the world, moving it forward in areas such as technology, medicine, political theory and the social sciences. We call this type of research *inquiry-based*, because research is all about asking questions.

Academics consider this never-ending process of asking questions and searching out answers as an ongoing *conversation*. Writing instructors like to describe the act of writing the academic essay as *entering the conversation* of academic inquiry. Now, when you hear the word "conversation", you probably immediately envision two people talking to each other, using their voices and the spoken word to communicate. This definition isn't wrong, but it is a limited characterization of the word.

When writing instructors refer to the ongoing conversation of academic inquiry, what we're really talking about is: 1) what's been previously said and written about a specific topic; 2) what's being said and investigated now; and 3) where the research might lead this specific topic in the future. As Green (2011) observed, "when we sit down to write an argument intended to persuade someone to do or to believe something, we are never really the first to broach the topic about which we are writing. Thus, learning how to write a researched argument is a process of learning how to enter conversations that are already going on in a written form" (p. 11). As writers, we consider our knowledge of the subject, compare it to what we've discovered in our research, and then draw conclusions or pose more questions for future consideration.

You are about to join a conversation that, in the eyes of teachers, professors, and scientists, never really ends. In an attempt to help college students better understand this concept, many scholars have referenced Burke's (1976) famous passage about entering a parlor. A philosopher who contributed to conversations in his field and many others, Burke created the following metaphor to illustrate how knowledge production and writing are not solitary endeavors, but instead social acts in which we participate. In *The Philosophy of Literary Form*, he wrote of a conversation going on in a parlor:

> You come late. When you arrive, others have long preceded you, and they are engaged in a heated discussion, a discussion too heated for them to pause and tell you exactly what it is about... You listen for a while, until you decide that you have caught the tenor of the argument; then you put in your oar. Someone answers; you answer him; another comes to your defense; another aligns himself against you... The hour grows late, you must depart. And you do depart, with the discussion still vigorously in progress. (pp. 110-11)

If you can't envision yourself in Burke's parlor, place yourself instead at an uncle's birthday party.

You leave campus to arrive a little late at Uncle Amir's house. Your dad and his brothers and sisters are debating whether their favorite baseball team will make the playoffs this year. This generation takes its sports seriously and their arguments are getting louder. You cut in, saying you think the team has a good chance because of the recent acquisitions of two power hitters. Uncle Tony pipes in and argues that winning isn't just about hitting, but instead it's all about the pitching. Your dad takes your side and spouts some batting statistics from last year. The argument continues over the dinner table, and you must leave before the birthday cake. The debate will continue the rest of the night, and throughout the rest of the summer.

By their very nature, academic essays demand that writers express ideas, but as writing instructors Graff, Birkenstein and Durst (2012) said, it's also the writer's responsibility to present ideas as a response to what others have said (p. 3). So if you were writing an essay about your family's baseball debate, you would introduce the idea, then provide the historical context of your family's baseball history. The essay would go on to describe how each uncle and aunt perceives baseball, what the current team looks like, and what your opinions are. The essay would wrap-up with "let's wait and see what happens this summer" —the result of considering all the information you just put forth: family opinions and love of the game, coupled with past and current performance statistics.

This is how an academic essay can work. Scholarly journal articles and credible internet websites help provide the writer with an understanding of what's been said. Every writer reads even more in the form of books and periodicals as she tries to understand the current conversation surrounding a particular topic, while she sees how her opinions fit in with all of this information.

Your response to this idea of entering the conversation might be "How can I do this? I've never done anything like this before." Here, I would say you are wrong. You have moved through this very process before, unaware that you were entering the conversation when, in fact, that is what you were doing. What do I mean by this?

Every day we enter into metaphoric conversations, every time we walk into a room or react to a situation. Our previous knowledge of these situations and on-the-spot research come together to help us figure out what to think, what to say, and how to act in many of our daily situations.

We may not be aware that we are constantly analyzing the situation as we are living it, but, as the example below illustrates, that is exactly what we are doing.

Late for Work

It's a Monday, and you overslept. You realize you now are late for work and you must quickly make an important decision: do you call into work sick, do you call work and tell your boss you are on your way, or do you just leave for work and not call at all, knowing you'll be late and hoping it will go unnoticed?

Even though you are unaware of your own thought process, you immediately begin to analyze how you will handle this problem based on the consideration of **audience, purpose** and **context. Audience,** in this instance, is the person you will call at work. Will you choose to talk to your boss or a coworker? Why would you choose one person over the other?

Next, you consider the **purpose** of your call. Will you try to make an excuse for being late and say you will be there soon? Will you tell the truth and say you overslept? Will you call in sick and take the rest of the day off?

Deciding which person you will call and what you will say includes a consideration of your overall work situation or the **context**. Have you called in sick or late before, or even recently? How will your boss react if you call in sick or late? What does your boss know about you and think of you? What do you know about your boss and how she will react to your telephone call? Determining the answers to these questions defines the context of the situation. This context can also include how far from work you live, what day of the week it is, what is going on at work that day, and what you anticipate might occur at work.

You might talk to someone else about your dilemma. You call your mom or ask your roommate for advice, and this advice informs the context. Then, after weighing all this information in the span of just a few minutes, you make a decision. You have decided on your audience: you will speak with a coworker.

The purpose of the call will be to say you know you are late but you are on your way. You made these choices based on what you knew about the context of the situation, which includes you, your boss, your coworkers and work.

You made an informed decision based on the knowledge and experience you have, and you effectively communicated your purpose to your audience. The very same thought process of considering past experience, coupled with current knowledge and future prognostication, is what needs to happen when you are making research and writing decisions in college and beyond.

By entering the conversation, you convey your understanding of your audience, the purpose of the written communication, and context of the variables involved. For the purposes of the academic research essays you will be writing at OU, your audience is the other writers to whom you are responding, the subject is the essay topic (chosen by you or your instructor) and the communication format is the academic essay.

The Rhetorical Situation

Understanding the audience and purpose of a communication is essential to becoming a more effective writer and communicator. In composition, **rhetoric** is the study of the strategies for using language effectively. Composition instructors call the situations writers encounter in their work—like the situation described above—the **rhetorical situation**. The deconstruction (the taking apart) of the situation, which we call the *rhetorical analysis*, provides answers to *the who*, *the what* and *the why* of any given event, assignment or topic. All of this might seem strange at first, but you just analyzed the **rhetorical situation** of waking up late for work, and you have actually been analyzing rhetorical situations your whole life.

Part of understanding how to "enter the conversation" includes applying the core composition ideas of context, audience and purpose of communication. Whenever a writer enters into academic research, he needs to understand the context of the subject matter, his potential audience, and what he hopes to accomplish with his writing. This idea of audience awareness is crucial to this writer successfully entering the conversation of his discourse community.

Although writing instructors like to focus on the written application of rhetorical analysis and entering the conversation, it is extremely helpful to understand what has happened, what is happening and what might happen, with regard to many situations you face as a college student, such as waking late for work.

To help you better understand the idea of rhetorical analysis as it pertains to writing, let's examine the common experience of the quickly disappearing tradition of the handwritten thank you note.

The Thank You Note

It's been a month since your last birthday and your Dad reminds you to write a thank you card to Grandma for the birthday gift she gave you. The rhetorical situation, or context, surrounding this thank you note would include the kind of relationship you have with Grandma, the reason for the note, and how you feel about the gift. The audience for the note would be, of course, your grandmother. You have known Grandma your entire life. You know what she values, and so that is one reason you are handwriting this note. She doesn't use a computer and doesn't text, so you know she values handwritten correspondence delivered via "snail mail."

The purpose of the note is clear. You need to thank her for the sweater. But besides the actual gift itself, the purpose of the note could also be to acknowledge her generosity, as well as to show her your love and respect. You have known your grandmother your entire life, and so therefore you are very aware of the rhetorical situation.

Your ability to fully analyze this rhetorical situation will enable you to make important decisions when composing your note. These decisions include the style of the language used in the note, the fact that the note is handwritten, and the timeliness of the note. You tell Grandma how much you like the sweater, using loving language to let her know you appreciate the time and money she invested in your gift. You choose a card with daisies on it, because you know they are her favorite flower. You sign it using her pet nickname for you. You write the note quickly and drop it in the mail the next day.

Again, without consciously knowing it, you have examined the rhetorical situation of writing Grandma a thank you note, and made important writing decisions based on that analysis.

The Rhetorical Situation of the Academic Essay

Now let's take these ideas of audience, purpose and context and apply them to your academic research essay. A typical WRT assignment at OU may ask you to observe one community of your choice and, using that observation, choose a focus or research question to pursue. For example, in response to this kind of assignment, you might elect to observe your place of work, a fast food restaurant, and then write about the link between America's growing obesity problem and fast food.

As a first-year composition student, you will soon learn to navigate the Kresge Library website, including its homepage, and use of the Library One database search engine. This is where you begin your quest to find out what's been said about your issue of obesity and fast food.

This is also where you will find out how substantial the conversations surrounding your topic are. In your first search, you discover that between 2000 and 2010 there were 10,000 scholarly articles written that contain the search terms "obesity" and "fast food." Immediately, it becomes clear that you can't possibly read everything that has been added to the academic conversation about obesity and fast food.

Of course, 10,000 articles is a huge research cluster, so you learn how to narrow your search terms and instead you end up with about 400 articles from scholarly journals, periodicals and trade publications.

You employ the reading strategies of skimming the publication titles, article titles, and the abstracts (summaries that appear before the articles) of the most intriguing 10 articles. As you read through the best articles, you begin to glimpse the issues involved and learn more about current trends in the thinking about fast food and obesity.

As you are reading, you also are simultaneously comparing your personal belief and previous knowledge of obesity and fast food. You then begin to see who agrees and disagrees with you. What you are doing is taking a source (what someone said about your topic in Article A) and relating it to your ideas and the other ideas you are discovering in this ongoing conversation of obesity and fast food. As Green (2011) said, "every argument you make is connected to another argument. Every time you write an argument, the way you position yourself will depend on three things: which previously stated arguments you share, which previously stated arguments you want to refute, and what new opinions and supporting information you are going to bring to the conversation" (p. 11-12).

You are now giving Article A (its author and ideas) some sort of meaning and importance by placing it in relation to other information, both your own and that which you have found through research. Graff, Birkenstein and Durst

(2012) advised writers to "listen carefully, including those who disagree with us, and then engage with them thoughtfully and respectfully" (p.14). Academic conversation is the art of listening and responding in a civil dialogue. This balanced and informed practice will serve you well in both your academic and professional communications.

Beyond the Classroom

Writing an academic essay will probably only take place for you during your college education, and graduate school, if you pursue it. But what happens once you graduate and move on to a job or career? How does this idea of entering the conversation fit in with "the real world"?

Consider this: you just graduated with an engineering degree and have secured your first job. It's your first week, and you are just now finding out where to park and eat your lunch, and you are learning the computer system. Your boss has just assigned you your first report. Where do you begin? Where do you look for information and with whom can you talk? By the time you complete OU's Writing Foundation class, WRT 160, this process should be familiar to you.

This is where you can apply the concept of rhetorical analysis. You now know you need to determine what's been previously said on your report topic, what you already know about the topic, and how the two might fit together. You proceed to review engineering articles and websites, read company manuals and the company website, consult with coworkers and your supervisor. Perhaps your research needs to incorporate a laboratory experiment, observations of a product's performance, or include an interview with an expert on your subject. Will your report need to just report the facts, or will you need to interpret the information and respond to it? You don't panic, because you've been through this process before.

Writing is challenging, as you well know, and your college professors will challenge you as you have never been challenged before. Engaging the ideas of others and responding to them, or entering into the conversation, is one of the most important concepts you will learn in college and it will help you make sense of your life, both in the real world and in your career or field. Just remember that your college professors, writing instructors and the OU Writing Center are here to help you. We want you to succeed and we know you will.

Questions for Further Discussion

1. Choose an everyday experience and try analyzing it rhetorically. Consider a situation from home, work or school. What task are you faced with or what needs to be accomplished? What is your previous experience with the situation, people and issues involved? What questions might you ask to gain more information and who would you ask? Where could you find more information? What would be the best way to implement your decision or reaction? What would be the purpose of your action and who would be recipient of this action? What will be the result from your action? Write out your rhetorical analysis and then share it with your group.

2. As a group, decide on a shared experience to analyze rhetorically, using the same criteria as described above. Negotiate the answers as a group, and share the group's findings with the class.

References

Burke, K. (1976). *The philosophy of literary form*. Los Angeles: University of California Press.

Graff, G., Birkenstein, C., & Durst, R. (2012). *They say/I say*. New York, NY: W.W. Norton and Co.

Green, S. (2011) Argument as conversation: The role of inquiry in writing a research argument. In E. Wardle & D. Downs (Eds), *Writing about writing: A college reader* (pp. 11-13). Boston, MA: Bedford/St. Martin's Press.

[9]

CRITICAL READING AND THINKING:
A How-To-Do-It Guide to Savvy Reading

Alice Horning

Welcome to college. You probably already know that much of what lies ahead of you entails reading. A lot of reading! This chapter of *Grizz Writes* is meant to help you understand the kinds of reading your instructors will expect you to do and to provide you with some specific strategies for doing that reading efficiently and effectively. Strong critical reading and thinking abilities are keys to success in college and beyond; all of us (teachers and students both) need to be better, faster readers. This chapter will offer you tools to develop these savvy reading abilities as you build reading expertise in and out of school, on paper and online.

Critical Reading and Thinking: You can DO THAT!

Reading is a skill everyone develops through practice with textbooks, news sources, magazines, novels, websites and all other kinds of writing. Research studies on both students like you and expert readers tell us some of the key characteristics of good reading. Good reading is fast; done efficiently, you should get everything you need from any text in one pass. When you are engaged in what you are reading, you not only get all the ideas the writers present, but you also make connections to other material and, in college, to what you are learning in class as well. Skills in savvy reading include active engagement with a text through focused, uninterrupted close attention to organization, key points, vocabulary, and evaluation. How can you do all of that and become a savvy reader?

The skills you need to pull off good reading are these: analysis, synthesis, evaluation and application. They are the skills of critical thinking, according to education researcher Benjamin Bloom, who proposed a taxonomy or framework for teaching purposes (Bloom & Krathwohl, 1956; revised by Krathwohl & Anderson, 1999) that can also be applied to effective and efficient reading. The rest of this chapter is devoted to describing strategies for the development and use of these skills.

Strategies for Analysis

Analysis means taking a text apart to see its structure and ideas. When you are reading easy material, you can analyze it without much effort. Textbook material, journal articles, historical documents, or scientific reports are more challenging because of their complicated structure, ideas, and unfamiliar vocabulary. But if you work at taking them apart, you can read them efficiently and effectively. To do so, you need to engage with the text in some active ways so that you do more than run your eyes over the lines of print. Your goal is to read a chapter or article once and get all of the key ideas presented by the author. Three strategies will allow you to achieve this goal.

Strategy 1: Look for the organizational structure of the text. As you begin to read, you should be thinking about the kinds of text structures that might captured in a visual diagram, such as one for a comparison-contrast text in Figure 1.

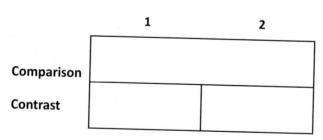

Figure 1. Comparison-contrast. Reprinted from *Reading in a second language*, by W. Grabe, 2009, Cambridge, MA: Cambridge University Press.

Diagrams like this one were developed by William Grabe, a professor at Northern Arizona University who teaches students whose native language is not English, to help students see the structure of English texts when they read. Even if English *is* your native language, visualizing these organizational patterns can help you see the main ideas being presented by a writer. So if your history text has a section called "Comparing the Causes of World War I and World War II," you can organize notes or text marking consistent with the diagram in Figure 1. If you are reading an argument, a diagram like the one in Figure 2 may help you analyze the structure of the ideas. These organizational patterns may also be familiar to you from discussions of different types of papers you may be writing in your Writing and Rhetoric course. This strategy should be useful when you are reading so you can see the structure of the text.

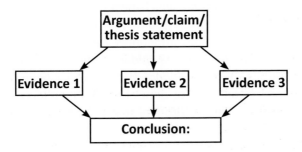

Figure 2. Argument. Reprinted from *Reading in a second language*, by W. Grabe, 2009, Cambridge, MA: Cambridge University Press.

Strategy 2: You can use visual diagrams like the ones here or ones of your own creation to take notes on any text. The diagram will allow you to find the main ideas within the structure, and also incorporate the details or examples or specific facts the author presents to support the main ideas. You have probably learned some other note-taking strategies, like double-column pages, or KWL (what I know, what I want to know, and what I learned). Taking careful notes using a diagram or another strategy does make reading more time-consuming, but once you've done those notes, you will not need to read the chapter again, saving you time and boredom!

Strategy 3: Complex texts like textbook material are complex in part because of the vocabulary. Any textbook that has *Introduction to* in its title is going to have a lot of new vocabulary for you to absorb. It will also have features to help you deal with the new words. Typical introductory textbooks will have a glossary of key terms, often at the back of the book. The words that appear in the glossary are usually marked in some way in the text: highlighting, bold type or definitions in the margins or at the bottom of the page are common. Using the glossary saves you the trouble of looking words up in the dictionary, either paper or online. Research with students like you, using results from the reading section of the ACT (remember that?) shows clearly that expanding your vocabulary is a key aspect of savvy reading.

But there will also be words you won't know that are not in the glossary. For these, you should first see if you can get the meaning from the context of the sentence and paragraph in which it appears. A second approach is to take the word apart and see if you recognize any of its parts. The word 'psychology,' for instance, has –ology at its end, which most people know means "the study of." The combination of recognizing some part of the word plus the context can often give you the meaning. Sometimes, neither context nor analysis of parts will be helpful and then, you should look the word up in a real diction-ary. A word of caution here: *dictionary.com* and other online resources will not always provide a complete or accurate definition, so you may want to make use of a printed college dictionary to get the full picture of words you don't know. Learning vocabulary specific to every discipline you study is part of your job as a college student. If you put in a focused effort, your vocabulary will expand quickly and you will find yourself with a steadily decreasing need to look up new words as you find them in reading.

Strategies for Synthesis

If you use the analytical strategies described above, you will have a good grasp of the structure and main ideas of everything you read. With those ideas in hand, you will be able to draw your readings together and synthesize what you have read for whatever purposes you might have. You might, for example, be writing a paper on an assigned topic in any course at the university that calls for the use of outside sources. But synthesis is an essential critical think-ing skill useful in life. If you were going to buy a car, for example, you might want to take a test drive, but you might also want to talk to friends who own the same or a similar car, and to a mechanic who has some experience main-taining or repairing the car you think you want. In addition, you might want to read about the car in published articles online or in a magazine like *Consumer Reports*, famous for its impartial evaluation of cars and many other products.

Having done this research, you would then be in a position to synthesize all the information to make your buying decision. Synthesis, then, entails taking material from a variety of sources and putting it together for a specific purpose, whether writing a paper, buying a car, advising your boss on a work situation, or a number of other situations. Synthesis builds on analysis.

So, how to do that? You can ask yourself a few key questions, building on your analysis of whatever you have read, to create a synthesis. In the car buying example, you might ask yourself if your friends and the mechanic agree or disagree, and on which points. You might ask if the sources are all using the same basis for their comments. You should think about which information seems most convincing to you and why. In asking these questions, you will also need to rely on your strategies for evaluation.

Strategies for Evaluation

Savvy readers evaluate everything they read, whether it is a magazine in the checkout line at the grocery store, or a website, or a book. Evaluation is essential to sort solid, valid, reliable information from hearsay, illusion and junk. The academic group that has done helpful work on evaluating sources is the Association of College and Research Libraries (ACRL), a subgroup of the American Library Association. This organization is the major professional group for library faculty like those you will meet at Kresge Library at Oakland. In its *Information Literacy Standards* (2008), the ACRL provides a good strategy for the evaluation of any source you might read. The strategy involves analyzing the material on these six criteria: authority, accuracy, currency, relevancy, bias and appropriateness. To use this strategy, ask yourself these questions as you read:

1. **On authority:** Who is the author of this piece and what are his or her qualifications? If the author is an organization, what kind of organization is it? If there is no author, where does the material come from? Your goal is to establish that the source has the knowledge and background to provide good information.

2. **On accuracy:** Does the material seem consistent with what else you know or have been able to determine about the topic or issue you are studying? If you have looked at several sources on the composition of moon rocks that describe their chemical

structure and you find a source that says the moon is made of green cheese, you should have doubts about the accuracy of this source.

3. **On currency:** When was the material published, posted online or most recently updated? This question is most important with web-based materials, but applies to print sources as well. For some topics, current information is essential, but for others, older material may also be useful, such as if you are doing some kind of historical survey or review. If you are reading about a serious illness, the most current information is the material you want, so currency is often an essential component of your evaluation.

4. **On relevancy:** Is this material really about the specific aspect of your topic you want to research? In research on a topic, you may find a lot of material that is about that topic, but only some of it will be relevant to the question you are trying to answer or the issue you are studying. For example, there are probably hundreds or thousands of books, articles and websites about Abraham Lincoln, but a much smaller number that focus on his Emancipation Proclamation. Evaluating for relevancy can help you limit and focus your reading to be more efficient and effective.

5. **On bias:** Does the material present a balanced view of the topic or issue? To evaluate for bias can sometimes be a challenge, especially if you are reading material that provides a viewpoint with which you agree. Watch for inflammatory language of any kind, and see if both pro and con positions are presented. If the writer says "another scholar examines this issue from the opposite point of view" or words to that effect, it is likely that you are getting a balanced presentation of the topic.

6. **On appropriateness:** Does what you are reading come from a reasonable source for your purpose? If you are reading the latest celebrity news online and are reading only for your own pleasure or information, that's fine, but if you are reading for a research report for a university course, the magazine at the gro-

cery checkout is probably not an appropriate source. Your goal is to consider your purpose for reading and decide if the text you are looking at is appropriate given your plans for its use.

Evaluation is an essential component of savvy reading. Like analysis and synthesis, a careful evaluation does take time, but the time is well spent doing a complete, careful reading of any text.

Strategies for Use

Using whatever you read for any purpose is the final strategy. For students in first-year writing, this use is most likely to be in papers you prepare for your courses, both those in Writing and Rhetoric and those in your other courses at Oakland. To use source materials appropriately in your written work, you may want to follow a plan shared with me by Catherine Haar, who regularly teaches all of our first-year courses. She suggests the following series of steps for every source you use:

Step 1: Introduce and qualify your source. If you have followed all of the steps outlined above, especially the evaluation strategies, you know that your source material is authoritative, accurate, current, and so forth. Your evaluation of the authority of the information is what you want to present when you introduce your source.

Step 2: Use a signaling tag. To indicate clearly that you are relying on a source before you present it, the signaling tag, like "According to Professor X, who has published 20 articles on this topic...". This phrasing provides your reader with information about the qualification of the source and indicates that you are now about to *use* what you have read.

Step 3: Present the source information. Here, you will rely on your analysis and perhaps also on your synthesis in your reading of the material you are presenting. You should be able to capture the main idea(s) and details provided by the source, and perhaps to incorporate, through synthesis, material from other sources. You should be able to present the source mostly in your own words (if you have done a thorough analysis), through summary or paraphrase. If the source has a particularly important or well-phrased section, that material might warrant direct quote. Make a conscious choice about the form in which you use your sources.

Step 4: Do something with the material. What you have read should fit into your argument or discussion, but you need to do the fitting. You should have something to say about the information you have read: probe, comment, add, compare to other sources, contrast, and argue. Do something with what you have read. You didn't do all that hard work of analysis, synthesis and evaluation for nothing! Make it work for you.

Step 5: Document your material. Provide an in-text citation to the source and give the full details about the source in proper form on your Reference list at the end of the paper.

Becoming a Savvy Reader

Reading is a lot of work; there are no two ways about it. But re-reading chapters and articles is also a lot of work, and it gets pretty boring to go over the same stuff. Research from ACT and other sources (Jolliffe & Harl, 2008; Hillesund, 2010) suggests that college students need better reading skills, and the strategies discussed here can help you become a more efficient and effective, savvy reader. The ACT study showed that many college students don't have the reading skills required for college success; savvy readers are more likely to do well in their courses and graduate. While the ACT Reading test is limited (you might recall that it was 40 multiple choice questions on four passages, with only 35 minutes to read and answer), a different study of untimed student reading also supports the need for students to improve their reading. In Jolliffe and Harl's examination of student reading journals, they found that students need to work harder on analysis and synthesis, especially focusing on putting reading material together with information and ideas from other sources (2008). They also point out that teachers can help students build skills in "electronic contexts" (2008, p. 614); being a savvy reader applies just as much on a screen as it does to books and other traditional printed material. Work with expert readers in a study of faculty reading (Hillesund, 2010) shows that expert readers have and use these skills in successful careers.

The savvy reading strategies offered here will serve you well in every course at OU, because being able to analyze, synthesize, evaluate and apply what you learn from reading is the key to college and professional success. You can also help yourself build stronger reading skills by reading a book (preferably on some nonfiction topic, that is, not a novel, but something you are really interested in) for fun every day, for at least ten minutes. In this daily reading, try to do two things: read a little faster than is comfortable, and don't let yourself get interrupted by anything. Sustained, immersive reading that is focused and fast will help you become an effective reader who can see text structure, get main ideas, handle vocabulary, and connect different texts on a topic or issue efficiently. Practice with all the strategies discussed here will make savvy reading second nature and will contribute to your success in every class as well as your career.

References

American College Testing. (2006, 1 March). *Reading between the lines: What the ACT reading test reveals about college readiness.* Retrieved from http://www.act.org/research/policymakers/reports/reading.html

Association of College and Research Libraries. (2008). *Information literacy competency standards for higher education.* Chicago, IL: ACRL. Retrieved from http://www.ala.org/acrl/standards/informationliteracycompetency

Anderson, L. W., & Krathwohl, D. R. (Eds.). (2001). *A taxonomy for learning, teaching and assessing: A revision of Bloom's Taxonomy of educational objectives: Complete edition.* New York: Longman.

Bloom, B. S. & Krathwohl, D.R. (1956). *Taxonomy of educational objectives: The classification of educational goals, by a committee of college and university examiners. Handbook 1: Cognitive domain.* New York: Longman.

Grabe, W. (2009). *Reading in a second language.* Cambridge, MA: Cambridge University Press.

Hillesund, T. (2010). Digital reading spaces: How expert readers handle books, the Web and electronic paper. *First Monday 15*(4). Retrieved from http://firstmonday.org/htbin/cgiwrap/bin/ojs/index.php/fm/article/view/2762/2504.

Jolliffe, D.J.& Harl, A. (2008). Texts of our institutional lives: Studying the reading transition: from high school to college: What are our students reading and why? *College English 70*(6), 599-617. Retrieved from http://www.jstor.org/stable/25472296.

Appendix A: Graphic Organizers

Reprinted from Grabe, W. (2009). *Reading in a second language.* Cambridge, MA: Cambridge University Press.

1) Definitions

	is a		that	

2) Comparison-contrast

	1	2
Comparison		
Contrast		

3) Cause-effect (in any number as is needed)

1. ☐ → ☐
2. ☐ → ☐
3. ☐ → ☐

4) Process/sequence

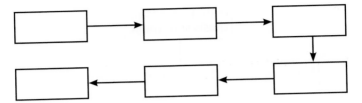

5) Problem-solution (in any number as is needed)

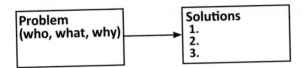

6) Description/classification

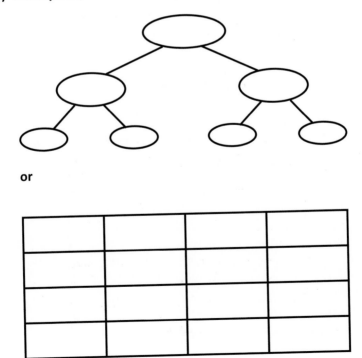

or

7) Argument

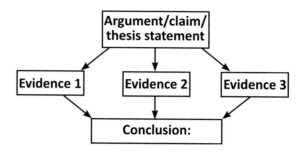

8) For-against (cf. comparison-contrast)

	for	against
Position 1		
Position 2		

[10]

IF YOU COULD ASK ANY QUESTION:
Introducing Open Inquiry-Based, Student-Centered Writing Projects

Ben Bennett-Carpenter

If you could ask any question about anything, what would that question be?

If you could say anything about anything (make a statement), what would you say?

Your response to one or both of these questions could be the beginning of a writing project that could be very interesting and/or useful for you. Think about it. Here at the university, you potentially may investigate any question within reason (and with the direction of your instructor). You potentially may make any statement within reason (and with the direction of your instructor). If you choose to pursue something that is interesting or useful to you now, this could be one of the most interesting or useful times of your life.

Many Oakland University writing instructors start with *you*—the student— and *your questions* or chosen topics. This approach to writing projects is what we call *open inquiry-based* and *student-centered*. In this chapter, I describe what an open inquiry-based project is, provide an example of the kind of open inquiry assignment you might encounter in an Oakland University writing course, and outline some reasons why your writing instructor may choose to use an open inquiry-based, student-centered approach to teach writing. Following the crucial questions in your life right now—through your writing projects—may lead to some of the most meaningful or significant work that you have ever done.

What is an Open Inquiry-Based Project? Basic Description and Example

A writing project or assignment that is "open" and "inquiry-based" means that it allows for any question that may be reasonably pursued. The word "inquiry" simply means the process of asking a question and pursuing a potential answer. Projects that are inquiry-based are not closed to questions but, rather, are welcoming of questions that may come or go from all sorts of angles. *Why is the sky blue?* A simple question like this could be the beginning of scientific research into why it is so. A question like *why do people keep secrets?* could lead to psychological, sociological, or cultural investigation (social sciences). *How does a person become creative?* could be the beginning of a project in the arts or humanities. Sometimes questions center on you as a person, such as: *How can I have the kind of relationship with a significant other that I want to have?* Or *what does it take for me to make it in my chosen future career?* Working with your instructor on questions like these—and a potentially infinite number of other questions— may lead to the pursuit of a focused, innovative writing project that is significant to you (and potentially to others as well).

Open inquiry, student-centered projects may take on various shapes and sizes, depending upon you and your instructor. Besides writing an essay or paper, the final product could include elements such as the ones listed below:

- conducting interviews or surveys
- attending events or investigating institutions
- analyzing media or books

- giving pre-professional quality poster displays and verbal presentations
- creating simple websites, blogs, or wikis
- creating presentations and/or discussion groups through social networking media
- making short videos/films
- writing in different genres: comics, creative non-fiction, editorials, etc.
- inventing games
- creating artwork or performing arts

One example of an open inquiry-based, student-centered project is given here as an assignment for a project proposal.

Project Proposal Assignment Sample

A project is any work, within reason, proposed by you and approved by the instructor that can be accomplished by the due date.

After brainstorming and perhaps doing some preliminary investigation on some possible ideas for your project, you will want to consider what you would really like to do or what would be useful to you.

As you compose your proposal, you should keep in mind that the project should be manageable and the quality should be high, though experimentation in an area that is new for you is also encouraged for this assignment.

You may propose a project as an individual or as a group.

In order for your project idea to be considered for approval, I want you to put together a proposal of approximately two pages or 500 words that includes as many of the following elements as applicable to your project idea. This may be in the form of an essay or simply a list that follows the checklist here. In your proposal, you will tell me:

- The question or issue that you are pursuing – this may be stated as a question or described as an issue or problem that you are attempting to solve. If you already have a potential answer for the question or you are ready to make a statement about it (you already know what you want to say about it), then do so.

- Possible title of the work (this is not set in stone – just give it a shot)

- One to two paragraph description of the project

- One paragraph describing why the project is interesting, significant, and/or useful to you

- A brief list of methods that you will be using

- At least one new thing that you are experimenting with, or developing, in the project

- Steps in the process in order to complete the project, including a preliminary timetable (If a group project, list which individuals will do what tasks)

- List three to five or more (3-5+) possible information sources for your project. These should be listed in bibliographic format like you would on a Works Cited or References page (MLA or APA).

- List the main point or points you would like to address in your writing (essay, paper, etc.). In other words, what do you think you will *say*? What statement do you have to make? If you are not sure, then just restate this point as the question, problem, or issue that you are pursuing.

- What activity-based investigation related to your topic do think you might do? Some examples of activity-based investigation include:

    - conducting formal or informal interviews (or both) with "people on the street," family members, friends, and/or experts/specialists

    - conducting surveys (online or "on the street" or both)

    - attending events and observing/documenting what is happening

    - investigating institutions by interviews, data analysis, and "field research"

    - self-discovery research through a volunteer "field experience"

    - digging through old archives, photos, objects, letters, etc., for information that will help you answer your question

- analyzing media or books (including art, film/movies, music, fiction, poetry, non-fiction, comic books, graphic novels, websites, etc.)

- Make a statement that affirms that you will get necessary permissions from people in order to conduct your research and follow proper protocols for research at the university.

- List any questions or concerns you have about successfully completing the project.

  Include in your proposal any other elements that would help give a sense of what you want to do.

This is just one example of one kind of open inquiry-based, student-centered assignment I regularly assign. Your course instructor may approach this kind of assignment differently, but my hope is that through this sample, you can begin to see that pursuing your own question and making your own statement—while challenging—can be quite rewarding. This kind of assignment is all about *you and your interests*.

Why Open Inquiry? Why Student-Centered? Reasons for this Approach to Writing Projects

Why, then, do some writing instructors take this approach to one or more of their writing assignments? Writing faculty may embrace an open inquiry, student-centered approach to writing instruction for a number of important reasons.

First, *open inquiry* (asking any question and pursuing it through investigation) is a fundamental starting point for all thought, research, and eventually knowledge. In philosophy, Socrates recognized ignorance as a basic state in which we humans find ourselves and, thus, we ask questions about the world. We "examine" ourselves (self-reflect, ponder, contemplate) in order to know ourselves better.

In the sciences, a state of ignorance or not knowing something—along with a state of wonder—leads to research and experimentation and, from there, to knowledge. In the arts, questions like "What if…?" lead to "novel constructions" —that is, new configurations of materials and concepts. By openly pursuing your question(s) and saying what needs to be said, you are participating in the essential elements of what brings about new knowledge and creative work.

Along with this open inquiry, *free speech* is recognized as a basic ingredient for our free, democratic society and a crucial part of our university. That is, one has to be able to pursue any question, within reason, and say anything, within reason—otherwise one runs the risk of blocking knowledge, institutionalizing ideologies, and replacing freedom with oppression. I say "within reason" here because we are not talking about making speech-acts that would be destructive to other people like yelling "fire" in a crowded movie theater. Also, a statement in a university setting must be substantiated by good argumentation and evidence. Yet by putting forth your question or making your statement, you have a chance to contribute to what constitutes a free, open society rather than an authoritarian, oppressive regime.

Also, recent studies in *intelligence* are in harmony with open-ended student-centered projects that capitalize on an individual's particular strengths. Among others, Gardner's (1983) theory of "multiple intelligences" points to a range of ways that people show competence in given areas. We all have abilities that show up in one or more particular areas rather than on one single intelligence or academic test (see also Hock, 2009, pp. 100-110). These "intelligences" include:

- linguistic intelligence (good with words)
- musical intelligence (ability with music)
- logical-mathematical intelligence (good at math &/or logic)
- spatial intelligence (keen sense of imagined and physical spaces)
- bodily-kinesthetic intelligence (good at sports or dance or related movement)
- interpersonal intelligence (good with people)
- intrapersonal intelligence (skilled at exploring one's own mind and emotions)
- naturalist intelligence (understands how nature works)
- existential intelligence (ability to explore questions of life, death, & meaning)

By being open to pursue your interests, you have an opportunity to capitalize on your strengths. Which one of the above best describes your strengths?

The idea of multiple intelligences is corroborated by studies in evolutionary psychology that suggest our brains developed in a "modular" fashion. In other words, various elements of your brain's current structure and operation evolved in order to adapt to particular problems given in the environment. Thus, specialized modules developed, which now inspire reflection on "multimodal" projects and assignments such as the project proposal listed as an example above (see also Herrington, Hodgson & Moran, 2009). That is, employing multiple media or methods seems to fit the way our brains really operate. Incorporating multiple elements into our writing projects fits naturally more so than "uni-modal" projects. Uni-modal work seems to place artificial restrictions on how each one of us naturally does things. Thus, openness to various topics and methods generally is encouraged by Oakland University writing instructors.

Many more reasons may be given for open inquiry projects that begin with you and your interests. These include discussions of *creativity, experiential learning, humanistic psychology, self-discovery research, self-directed learning,* and *interdisciplinary studies.* But, when all is said and done, Oakland University writing faculty are committed to your "engagement and choice" in your writing projects for the sake of "authentic intellectual work" (NWP & Nagin, 2006, p. 48, 49).

As Elbow (2000) puts it:

- It is possible for anyone to produce a lot of writing with pleasure and satisfaction and without too much struggle.

- It is possible for anyone to figure out what he or she really means and finally get it clear on paper [or screen].

- It is possible for anyone to write things that others will want to read.

- Teachers can empower students, help them to like to write, and be more forceful and articulate in using writing in their lives. (as cited in NWP & Nagin, 2006, p. 18)

What do you think?

One of the best projects or assignments you can do is one that starts with *you* ("student-centered") and *your questions* ("inquiry-based"). If you ask the research question or pose the problem to be solved, you will find that your writing and critical thinking skills may develop light years ahead of where they would be otherwise. Because the source of an open-inquiry project is you yourself, an automatic self-adjustment may take place for you in regard to the work you are about to tackle. In so doing, whether you are aware of it or not, you may self-position your ability, desire, and openness to knowledge toward something that is distinctive—possibly a writing project that could not have been written by anyone else in the world but you.

In addition, the ability to identify crucial questions, investigate them, and compose statements that are substantiated by sound argumentation, reasons, and evidence is an ability that likely will serve you well as you continue in your chosen major and career. If you can do this in your Oakland University writing course, then you may be able to do it in your courses in science, arts, humanities, education, business—or whatever field you pursue. These abilities potentially make us all better citizens and people who may be able to cooperate better in a fast-shrinking world.

A project that starts with you and *your questions—whatever they may be—* (and proceeds to facilitate your marshalling of any potentially useful resources) could lead to one of the best semesters you have ever had. Welcome to the freedom, challenge, and potential of the university!

Questions for Further Discussion

1. If you could ask any question about anything, what would you ask?

2. If you could say anything (make a statement), what would you say?

3. What advantages and disadvantages do you see to an open inquiry-based writing project?

4. Which of Gardner's "multiple intelligences" do you think you have the most? Why?

5. Do you agree with Elbow's statements? Why or why not?

6. What might stop you from really pursuing something this semester that is interesting and/or useful to you?

References

Elbow, P. (2000). *Everyone can write: Essays toward a hopeful theory of writing and teaching writing.* New York: Oxford.

Gardner, H. (1983). *Frames of mind: The theory of multiple intelligences.* New York: Basic.

Herrington, A., Hodgson, K., & Moran, C. (Eds.). (2009). *Teaching the new writing: Technology, change, and assessment in the 21st-century classroom.* New York: Teacher's College; Berkeley, CA: The National Writing Project.

Hock, R.R. (2009). *Forty studies that changed psychology: Explorations in the history of psychological research.* Upper Saddle River, NJ: Pearson/ Prentice Hall.

National Writing Project [NWP], & Nagin, C. (2006). *Because writing matters: Improving student writing in our schools.* Revised and updated edition. San Francisco: Jossey Bass.

[11]

INTERVIEWING TECHNIQUES:
What to Do Before, During, and After

Marilyn Borner and Jenna Katz

Introduction

The purpose of interviewing is to find answers to questions you have regarding your research. What makes an interview most beneficial is that you can seek answers to questions you were either unable to find in your secondary research, or that you can only obtain from the first-hand knowledge of an expert. Whether you are conducting an interview for WRT 102, WRT 150, or WRT 160, your goal is the same: to ask effective questions that produce results you can use in your writing.

Conducting your first quality interview can be intimidating. You may have to talk to someone you have never met and ask questions, hoping that the responses will be useful for your paper. You may wonder what questions you are supposed to ask, if you should probe when you do not elicit a response you can use, and if you should follow-up for clarification. After the interview, you may find yourself wondering how to use the information you've obtained.

This chapter will show you what to do before, during, and after the interview in order to equip you not only to conduct a successful interview, but also to be able to use it effectively in your writing.

Before the Interview

Understanding the Assignment

The first step involved in any research is understanding the assignment. In order to ensure you know what is being asked of you, it is important to read and understand the assignment description, making sure that you ask your instructor questions prior to beginning your research. Be sure to read any resources your instructor has given for the assignment. It is also helpful to discuss your topic with your instructor prior to getting started to ensure that you are embarking on research for a topic that is acceptable.

Finding Someone to Interview

Step #1: Once you are ready to begin your primary research, the first step is finding credible sources to interview. There are a few ways you can go about this. One way is to discover the best person to talk to regarding your topic. In order to do this, you should think of what point of view is currently missing from your research. (Refer to the "Sources as Perspectives" chapter of *Grizz Writes* in order to determine the points of view necessary for a well-rounded argument.) For example, if you were researching why the high school drop-out rate is so high in a given area, you may wish to interview a high school advisor who works with students everyday who are at risk of dropping out or failing. Or, if you are researching what it would take to start a small business, you could interview a small-business owner or a business professor on campus. You'll want to interview someone who can provide information based on experiences that you couldn't get from your secondary sources. You may need to ask around. Ask your instructor, your friends, parents, co-workers, and other instructors.

Step #2: After you have identified potential interviewees (the person you will interview), then the second step is to obtain contact information. If the person you wish to interview works at Oakland, use the OU directory. If your interviewee works elsewhere, conduct an Internet search using a name and occupation, or you could use the site LinkedIn.com

Step #3: Before contacting your potential interviewee, the third step is to read a little bit about the source if the information is there for you. Interviewing is just like meeting anyone else for the first time; it helps if you have some background.

Contacting Your Interviewee

After you identify whom you will contact for the interview, it is a good idea to understand the purpose of your primary research and why you are contacting that source specifically. It might also be a good idea to jot down some questions that you will ask. You will want to focus your questions regarding the interviewee's expertise, training, and experience. When you call or email to set up the interview, you might be asked what types of things you wish to discuss, so it is wise to have a few things in mind. You should wait to finalize your list of questions until you know whether or not the interview will proceed as your questions will most likely change depending on the person you interview.

The next thing that is important prior to contacting your interviewee is having a list of dates and times when you are available for a phone or in person interview and when you will need their responses if you are conducting an interview via email. Be sure to give yourself enough time to follow-up after the interview by choosing a date that is earlier than the due date your instructor has given you for the project.

The last thing you need to do prior to requesting an interview is write down what you are going to say when you introduce yourself. This may sound silly to you now, but you may be nervous or distracted when on the phone, and you'll want to come across as professional as possible. Your source will take you seriously if you take the interview seriously. You should state:

- your name
- your reason for calling
- what your request is
- how many questions you will ask
- how long the interview will last

Your introduction could go something like this:

Hello, my name is _____ . I am currently researching _____ for my WRT _____ course at Oakland University, and I heard you were an expert in _____ . I am hoping to interview you regarding your knowledge and expertise. Is this something you would be available to do?

Deciding Which Method to Use to Interview

There are many ways to conduct an interview. In-person interviews will provide a more personal approach, but they may not always work into your or your source's schedules. If necessary, try a Skype or FaceTime interview or even email questions to your subject if no other form of communication will work.

Regardless of your method, if your source agrees to conduct the interview with you, then the next thing to do is establish when, where, and how the interview will be conducted. For in-person or over the phone interviews it is best to ask your source about their availability and be flexible with your own time. If the interview will be conducted via email, be sure you confirm the email address.

Obtaining Permission

A permission slip should be signed by all participants for any type of primary research you conduct. Here is a template you can use:

I _____ (interviewee's name) give _____ _____ (student's name) permission to use our interview in his or her research for Oakland University.

_____ (signed by interviewee)

During the Interview

A rhetorically savvy interviewer should be aware of how to make the best impression on an audience. For example, the day of the interview, you may want to think as much about what you will learn from the interviewee as what they might learn about you. If the interview is to be conducted in an office, hospital, or academic setting, it may be best to dress a bit more formally. If the interview is to be conducted in a more casual work environment, like in a restaurant kitchen, on a construction site, or at a plumbing supply company, you should probably dress more casually. People often feel more comfortable sharing professional opinions with people whose professional appearance more closely resembles their own.

Your professionalism (appropriate to the rhetorical situation) should shine through from the first handshake with your source. As Newhall (2009), points out, "[u]nprofessional interview behavior will jeopardize [a] reputation." In turn, it is usually a good idea to have specific and clear questions to ask. These insights also apply to Skype or video interviews: remember that the person on the other end of the computer can see you and everything you do. Effective interviewers are also aware of their facial expressions, and whenever possible, they look up from their notes and make eye contact with their subjects.

The first 30 seconds will often set the tone for the entire interview. DiCicco-Bloom and Crabtree (2006) argue that "[u]nlike the unstructured interviews used in traditional ethnography where rapport is developed over time, it is necessary for the interviewer to rapidly develop a positive relationship during [an] in-depth interview" (p. 316). It is not as easy as many may think to find common ground with an interview subject. However, there are strategies that you can use to make interviewees feel at ease and interested in sharing their insights. For example, consider engaging them in conversation. This may take some finesse, but it is possible to break the ice with some casual conversation about common interests, and doing so may set a good tone for the interview.

Stating Your Intentions

It is best to begin the interview by describing your research project to your source, and explaining what you'd like to learn more about and how the interviewee can help you to understand the subject matter. Even if you've read all that you can on the project and you feel like an expert, take the approach of learner at this point in the interview.

Always keep in mind that the purpose of the interview is to obtain information that is not published elsewhere. Your interviewee is someone with a specific skill set or knowledge base because of personal experience, so you should be sure to acknowledge that expertise.

Also, if you volunteer all of the information that you're trying to corroborate, it may create two negatives: 1) you may appear snobbish or egocentric and 2) you won't get the meaningful quotes and significant insights you are seeking from your interview subject.

Recording the Interview

Sometimes it's a good idea to record your interview. Recording can be very beneficial, especially if your handwriting is a little sloppy and you have trouble reading your own notes. It can also serve to promote accuracy in quoting your source.

You should always ask permission before recording an interview; however, even if they agree to be recorded, some people may not feel at ease with a recorder on the table. Keep in mind Al-Yateem's (2012), observations: "I noted that when I did not record interviews, communication tended to be less formal, more sociable, and more spontaneous." If you do intend to use a recorder, let your source know that the only purpose for the recording is to help you transcribe your notes so that you can quote him or her accurately. Assure your source that the recording will be destroyed immediately after your paper is written.

Although interviews are typically transcribed verbatim and may even be included as an appendix with the final paper, you should check with your instructor for specific guidance on how to deal with transcriptions.

Asking Good Questions

When determining what questions to ask, you can work with your professor, your peers, or the Writing Center to come up with a list of relevant questions. However, don't feel you have to ask every single question. When it comes to the questions, depending on the nature of the assignment, you should remember that you are not trying to argue your whole paper through the interview. Instead, you should be prepared to ask questions the source can answer based on their experience/expertise with the topic.

To get quality information from your sources, you should endeavor to ask primarily open-ended questions, questions that require a response aside from a simple "Yes" or "No." Investigative interviews often focus on how something works or why it occurs. Other ways to open a question might include the phrases "Tell me about…" or "Describe for me…" Below are some further examples of how a closed-ended question can be converted to an open-ended one.

Closed-Ended Question	Open-Ended Question
Do you think small businesses can be successful? ("Yes" or "No")	How do you think small businesses can be successful?
Do you have experience with financial records? ("Yes" or "No")	Tell me about any experience you've had with financial records.
Is there much writing done in the nursing field? ("Yes" or "No")	What type of writing is typically done in the nursing field?
Is it typical for you to engage in public speaking opportunities? ("Yes" or "No")	Can you tell me about the type of public speaking you do?

Maintaining Interview Etiquette

- Effective interviewers rarely interrupt their subjects mid-sentence. Instead, they wait until there's a pause in the conversation to go on to the next question. As Leech (2002) puts it, "One of the most important rules about asking questions has to do with shutting up. Give your respondent room to talk. If respondents get off topic, let them finish, then bring them gently back to the issue you are interested in. But don't try to control too much or you may miss important, unexpected points" (p. 668).

- Experienced interviewers have learned how to appear objective and non-judgmental. They begin by treating their sources the way they might treat someone they genuinely care about. Even when these interviewers observe their source's personal quirks (he's wearing one red sock and one blue) or it appears that the source is mistaken or not telling the truth, they keep this information to themselves and, if necessary, they may simply record their impressions in their notes.

- Interviewers can make their sources more comfortable by looking them in the eye and appearing to be genuinely interested in what their sources are saying. They use their body language to convey interest, such as leaning forward, taking notes, smiling, and nodding in agreement.

- The most effective interviewers pay close attention to what is being said and rarely worry about what their next question will be. More often than not, the next question will emerge as a logical result of what has just been said.

- Even the best interviewers occasionally have trouble moving the interview along. In those cases where there is an awkward or extended silence, they encourage their subjects by asking for clarification or by saying, "that's interesting. Can you tell me more?"

- And even when it seems unusually formal, effective interviewers tend to address their interviewees with formal titles: "Dr. Smith," or "Professor Johnson," for example.

After the Interview

As the interview concludes, you might find that your subject wishes to make a "front door confession." In many instances, the best nuggets of information can come after the interview has ended, as you're saying goodbye. It may be a good idea to end with the question, such as "Is there anything else you'd like to tell me?" At that point, you may find a bit of wisdom that you never thought to ask about. In some cases, you may even find information that might be intriguing, shocking, or scandalous. Often, subjects really want to provide information, but are hesitant until the very last minute.

Thanking Your Source

Upon completing the interview, thank your subject for taking the time to meet with you. Assure him or her that he or she did a good job and that the information provided will help your research. You can follow this up with an email of thanks, a small card, or a short note.

Opening Doors for Future Contact

Remember to ask if it would be okay to contact the source in the future if you need clarification or more information. Sometimes, after transcribing your notes, you may find that you're missing some key element of your research that a short phone call or email can provide. If you've left the door open for the possibility of re-contacting your source, you may not need to schedule another appointment and your subject may likely be more apt to provide you with a few more minutes of his or her time.

Using Your Results in Your Writing

The information you learn from your interview will be incorporated like any other source material into your essay. The interview may be introduced and cited as your source just as you would any other research that you incorporate into your paper (following either MLA or APA guidelines).

For example, as a result of an interview from a high school guidance counselor, you have a direct quote explaining that "The reason the high school dropout rate is so high is due to students needing to provide income for their families in this area." You had previously corroborated this information through a secondary source from John Smith (2014). You don't need to use a quote from a source simply to reiterate what you found from a secondary source; therefore, you wouldn't write:

> John Smith (2014) stated that many students drop out these days because they have to provide for their families. In my interview, Counselor Jones said, "The reason the high school dropout rate is so high is due to students needing to provide income for their families in this area."

Instead, you might use a paraphrase of this quote and list both sources in your in-text citation:

> Many high school dropouts today are prompted by students who need to provide support for their families and need to work (F. Jones, Personal communication, March 12, 2015).

As with all of the sources you use in your paper, you should be certain to use your interview to support what you say by quoting, paraphrasing, and summarizing that soure information correctly. It is best to use direct quotations sparingly because these are reserved for notable phrases or insights. Elements that are just informational and less engaging to readers might be better handled with paraphrase.

Sample Interview Exercises

1. Sit with a partner and role play the opening moments of an interview, as if the two of you had never met. Be professional and try to "warm up" your source in 30 seconds or less.

2. Prepare a list of questions for research and "practice" an interview with a student in your class or a friend. Jot down any possible problems you might encounter in a real interview situation. Be aware of closed-ended questions and the "yes" or "no" responses they will generate.

3. Prepare a list of questions for research and exchange them with someone else in your class working on a similar project. Peer review the questions, offering feedback on whether or not the questions meet all of your needs for research. Modify your questions if they did not meet your research needs.

References

Al-Yateem, N. (2012). The effect of interview recording on quality of data obtained: a methodological reflection. *Nurse Researcher, 19*(4), 31. Retrieved from http://nurseresearcher.rcnpublishing.co.uk/

DiCicco-Bloom, B., & Crabtree, B. F. (2006). The qualitative research interview. *Medical Education, 40,* 314-321. doi: 10.1111/j.1365-2929.2006.02418.x

Leech, B.L. (2002). Asking questions: Techniques for semistructured interviews. *PS: Political Science and Politics, 35,* 665-668. Retrieved from http://www.jstor.org/stable/1554805

Newhall, S. (2009). Research topic: Interview technique. *People Management, 15*(8), 44. Retrieved from http://www.cipd.co.uk/pm/default.aspx

[12]

VISUAL RHETORIC:
Reading the world around you

Jill McKay Chrobak

> *Our vision, our texts, our rhetoric are never neutral; our minds do not function in a vacuum devoid of subjectivity, political agendas, and points of view.*
>
> — Carolyn Handa (2004)
>
> *To be able to name one's experience is part of what it means to "read the world" and to begin to understand the political nature of the limits and possibilities of life within larger society. To be literate is not to be free; it is to be present and active in the struggle for reclaiming one's voice, history, and future.*
>
> — Jabari Mahiri (2004)

I saw the circle before I saw the kid in the middle. I was nine years old, the summer of 1978, and Marcy was my world. The shadowy bench-lined inner pathways that connected the twenty-seven six-story buildings of Marcy Houses were like tunnels kids burrowed through. Housing projects can seem like labyrinths to outsiders, as complicated and intimidating as a Moroccan bazaar. But we knew our way around.

– Jay-Z (2010)

Close your eyes and imagine yourself in the place Jay-Z describes above. What do you see? Do you notice the buildings first, the other kids, the maze of sidewalks? What does this place mean to you? What kinds of emotions are evoked when you picture such a space, place and time?

Chances are—even though Jay is extremely detailed in his description of this moment in time—that you will picture it differently. You may focus more on the people than the place or vice versa. His likening the Marcy Houses to a Moroccan bazaar may make you think of vibrant colors, stalls selling exotic spices, a land perhaps culturally foreign to you—or not. Viewing, like writing, is subjective—because as individuals we make judgments based on who we are personally, culturally, ethnically, racially, religiously, and socio-economically.

What is important in this exercise is not what you see but why and how you see it. That is, everything we see, just like everything we read and write, has an argument. As writing students at Oakland University, your instructors will expect you to not only be able to recognize and craft written arguments but to analyze and create visual arguments as well.

To say we live in an increasingly visual world would be a gross understatement. You are the Facebook generation, the digital generation, the "constantly barraged with images trying to get you to do/be/buy something" generation. But how often do you stop to think about what these images/artifacts are arguing? You'd be surprised how often you "analyze the visual" without even knowing it. This chapter will help you sharpen those skills, to recognize and analyze visual rhetoric as effectively as possible.

What is visual rhetoric?

Visual rhetoric . . . might be defined as a discipline that focuses on the visual elements that persuade . . . culture, along with images, sounds, and space, work together rhetorically to convince an audience.

– Carolyn Handa (2004)

Simply put, if rhetoric is the art of using language effectively, then visual rhetoric is the art of using images and/or artifacts effectively. Images are anything you can see: pictures, artwork, advertisements, signs, and symbols. Artifacts are anything you can touch: furniture, clothing, accessories, cars, and buildings. It is important for us as consumers, as viewers, as humans to be aware of the arguments that are being made around us on a daily basis.

For academic purposes, visual rhetoric is a vital component in most writing classrooms. You need to be able to recognize, analyze, and understand the visual arguments that surround you in order to craft effective and supportable rhetorical arguments of your own.

You should now have a pretty clear understanding of what visual rhetoric is in theory but it's important to discuss visual rhetoric in practice. For example, the most common and aggressive forms of visual rhetoric are advertisements. Whether it is an ad for clothing, food, or make-up they are all attempting to do the same thing: persuade you to buy whatever it is they are selling. These advertisers will spend countless hours assessing their audiences (who they envision will want to buy their product) and how best to visually persuade them to do so. Advertisers will agonize over what color of pink will be most vibrant to sell a lipstick, find the most famous movie star they can afford to model their product, and fight for days over how to situate the most delicious looking hamburger and fries on a plate. All of these design and image choices are carefully thought out with a specific purpose and audience in mind to achieve the end result of getting you, the consumer, to stop and look, to take notice of this advertisement and perhaps even be persuaded to buy the particular product they are selling. If the advertisers are in fact able to do this, then they are employing effective visual rhetoric.

Another example of visual rhetoric we see daily is signs and symbols. Something as mundane as a stop sign or as iconic as a professional sport's team's logo is steeped in visual rhetoric. When you see a stop sign you are surely "persuaded" to stop your car lest you want to get in a car accident. The stop sign is a symbol that speaks to you, that uses a symbol effectively to argue "Stop!" The Detroit Red Wing's symbol is iconic to most hockey fans and arguably anyone who lives in or around the Detroit area. The red bird's wing attached to a red wheel on a white background translates literally as the symbol of Detroit's hockey team, emblazoned on all the player jerseys and team merchandise. The symbol to most Detroiters literally argues "hockey team". However, many would argue that there are embedded arguments within the visual rhetoric of that symbol, that it effectively portrays much more than just a hockey team.

Analyzing Visual Rhetoric

This is where visual rhetoric gets really interesting, the analysis. Sticking with the sports teams as an example, let's analyze the Oakland University basketball team's logo. We can dig deeper to analyze what embedded arguments are rhetorically at play by answering the following list of questions:

- What is the first thing you notice when looking at this image/artifact?
- What does the choice of design argue about the image/artifact?
- What feelings does this image/artifact evoke from the audience? Does it make you sad, angry, happy, curious, etc.?
- Who do you think the intended audience is? Why?

- What do you think is the intended message or overall argument of this image/artifact? Explain.

- What does this image argue about society, culture, race, sexuality, and/or class in America?

- How does the image or artifact appeal ethically, logically or emotionally to the intended audience? Explain.

- Finally, and most importantly, does this image/artifact work? Is it effective? Does it succeed in doing what it is intended to do?

The following is how I would rhetorically analyze the logo as a visual text: First, I see the grizzly bear and then I notice the shading and contrasting colors are meant to define the musculature of the bear. I assume this is to make him look fierce, which is an embedded argument that alludes to the ferocity of OU's basketball team on the court. The colors are in the same shades as the school colors, though they are noticeably darker, perhaps to lend the image a greater sense of strength and boldness. I would argue that the audience for this symbol is primarily the OU student body and community and secondarily the greater pool of viewers who watch college sports. The purpose of this image is to be a symbol or an icon for Oakland University, so that when people view it they know exactly which school, which team, and which mascot is being represented.

Overall, I find the image to be effective because I know that every time I see it, or people in the tri-county area surrounding the university see it, they recognize it as the OU symbol. One could argue the image brings to mind whatever that person thinks about OU itself (it's a reputable university, they know someone who goes there or they go there themselves). These would be considered embedded arguments, or arguments that are subjective to the viewer's interpretation.

Again, this is my analysis and yours may very well be different. There are no right or wrong answers when it comes to visual rhetorical analysis. When you "read" an image, just as you read a text, we all have different interpretations. This is largely due to the fact that we are naturally beholden to a "complex web of subjectivities" (Strauss, 2003, p.730), that mix of family, religion, culture, race, ethnicity, sexual orientation and aesthetic preferences that make us individuals and how we see the world differently.

Learning to work with these subjectivities is imperative to critically analyzing the visual world around you, to make sense of what these visuals are arguing and to prove your interpretation to your desired audience. As writing students you need to be able to tap into your own unique perspectives in order to craft original and effective visual arguments. This means that when you analyze an image or artifact you are looking to prove your interpretation to an audience as well and therefore you need proof. You can bolster your argument about the image or artifact by using your answers to the guiding questions above as support, much like you would use research or quotations from credible sources to support your argument in an academic essay.

Recognizing and Crafting Effective Visual Arguments

Now that you have some tools to decipher visual arguments, it is important to discuss how you can create effective visual arguments of your own. Almost every notable writer has a favorite author or a signature way of writing. They are no different from you. And you, no doubt, have favorite visuals (pictures, images, places, colors, artifacts) that you find particularly appealing. To recognize what you find visually appealing is the first step in crafting effective visual arguments of your own. For some, this may mean developing a webpage that displays your academic and personal work. For others, this means putting together a personal style or outfit every day that presents to the world your particular tastes and preferences. Either way, crafting effective visual arguments means you need to first ask yourself: what do I want to say (argument) and to who do I want to say it (audience)?

To be more specific, consider the following questions when designing your own visual arguments:

- Who is your audience and what kinds of images would persuade them?

- What is your purpose with the image?

- What colors will elicit what kinds of responses from viewers?

- How will you illustrate ethos with your image?

- What, if any, emotional appeals do you want to make with this image?

- Would logic factor into your composition of this visual design?

By answering these questions you will be able to account for perhaps the most important factor to consider in crafting visual arguments: your audience. After all, no text—written or visual—is created in a vacuum. They all have a purpose and most often that purpose is to appeal in a particular way to a particular audience. If you are always mindful of your audience then your appeals will be that much more effective and clear.

After you have established who your audience is and what you want to argue, then it's time to start getting creative. When you are working to design an effective visual argument (a Facebook profile, a personal or professional website, an advertisement, a PowerPoint presentation, an informative Moodle space) one way to begin is by using Robin Williams's (1994) CRAP heuristic (contrast, repetition, alignment, proximity) printed below. This is a tool that can help you learn to recognize arguments embedded within the page and not just the prose. Contrast, repetition, alignment, proximity, and font choices contain deliberate arguments for intended audiences that warrant careful consideration and rhetorical analysis. The following list of questions can guide you to both recognize and craft effective visual arguments.

Contrast.

How do some of the words in this text contrast with each other? What colors are apparent and how do they compare? Are some words bigger or smaller than others? Are some parts of the text darker or lighter and more or less colorful? What does contrast portray to the audience? (Williams, 1994)

Repetition.

What aspects of the text are repeated? Why? What affect does this have on the audience? Why would an author or creator want to include repetition in the text? (Williams, 1994)

Alignment.

How is the text aligned on the page? Is it uniform? Is it formatted oddly? What do these alignment choices say about this text? How does the way the text is situated on the page suggest various appeals to the audience? (Williams, 1994)

Proximity.

How are the words spaced on the page? Are they close together or far away? What is the author or creator trying to achieve by placing the text this way?

Are some parts of the text separate from others? If so, why? If not, why not? What does how or where the text is located (in relation to other parts of the text on the page) say about the author or creator's intentions? What does this portray to the audience? (Williams, 1994)

Again, being conscious of your audience and the overall argument you are trying to portray is key to visual rhetoric. You need to be able to clearly and effectively persuade your audience to see your point of view and perhaps convince them of a particular point you are trying to prove. Using the CRAP heuristic can help you make sure your text and images are clearly getting your point across to your desired audience. Just like in effective written rhetoric, it is important to make sure your points are clear, concise, and well-developed. No one wants to read a messy, disorganized essay and it's safe to say that no one is persuaded by distracting and unappealing visuals.

The CRAP heuristic is meant to be a consideration for helping you to design and analyze effective visual arguments, but it is by no means absolute. It is important to note that other variables like color, texture, size, foreground and background should also play into your analysis as well. For example, if I were to craft a more complete visual rhetorical analysis of the OU basketball logo presented earlier, I would discuss more specifically the font used for the OU lettering. I believe the specific type of blocked and bold font was chosen to most clearly display the letters that represent Oakland University. If they were printed in a flowing script font they may be hard to read or perceived as "too girly" and would surely lose the "fierce and strong" message about OU's basketball team that the creators are trying to translate to the audience.

Furthermore, if I wanted to "read" the logo for embedded arguments about gender stereotypes, I would say that the font is markedly masculine because our society generally views men as physically stronger than women. Therefore, it is no surprise that the creators of the logo would want to craft a logo that proves to the audience the team's strength and physicality.

Understanding what visual rhetoric is and how to analyze images and artifacts rhetorically is an important skill in our increasingly technology-dependent world. By employing effective visual rhetoric you will be able to persuade your audience to actually *see* your point of view. Using the guiding questions and CRAP heuristic above, you can more easily navigate these analyses and begin to create appealing images and artifacts for a wide range of academic, personal and professional purposes.

Questions for Further Discussion

1. What is the most visually appealing thing you've ever seen? What made it so special, interesting, or appealing to you? Explain in detail. In your answer be sure to discuss WHY you think this thing is attractive to YOU. What does it say about what you value and believe in your life?

2. In groups, share your earliest memories of photography. Were they positive or negative, and why? When discussing your experiences, attempt to make a list of 5 reasons why we take and circulate pictures. What does the list say about our society?

3. What is your favorite song? Find the lyrics and design them using the CRAP heuristic as a guide. Play with MS Word, different font faces, colors and images to creatively portray the words of your favorite song *as* image. That is, you should represent your interpretation of the lyrics through visual means. When you are done with your design, explain to your audience why you chose to design them in that way. What colors did you use and why? What fonts were chosen, and why? What images did you choose, and why?

4. Below is a picture of the original OU mascot, Pioneer Pete. Conduct a visual rhetorical analysis of this logo by answering the questions listed under the OU Basketball team's logo. When you complete your analysis, compare its effectiveness with the current logo. Which logo is more rhetorically effective? Why do you think the mascot or logo was changed? Which do YOU find more appealing and why?

References

Handa, C. (2004). *Visual rhetoric in a digital world: A critical sourcebook.* New York, NY: Bedford/St. Martins.

Jay-Z. (2010). *Decoded.* New York, NY: Spiegel & Grau.

Mahiri, J. (2004). "New literacies in a new century." In J. Mahiri (Ed.), *What they don't learn in school: Literacy in the lives of urban youth.* (pp. 1-20). New York, NY: Peter Lang.

Strauss, D.L. (2003). "Photography and Belief." In R. Norgaard (Ed.), *Composing knowledge: Readings for college writers.* (pp. 728-735). New York, NY: Bedford/St. Martins.

Williams, R. (1994). *The non-designer's design book: Design and typographic principles for the visual novice.* Berkley, CA: Peachpit Press.

[13]

SOURCES AS PERSPECTIVES:
A Guide to Engaging and Critical Secondary Research

Christina Moore

At universities, *research* holds promising, adventurous, motivating, and even moral connotations: research empowers us to investigate difficult questions, evaluate false beliefs, and shine a light on injustices through diverse systems of proof. Ultimately, your professors are less interested in how you remember research information than how you *use* research to solve a problem or improve a condition. Therefore, OU's first-year writing courses will likely have a research writing assignment that calls you to investigate a topic using primary and secondary research.

Let's pose a research question that you could answer to improve a condition: "Would more federal regulation on plant-based food production reduce food contamination?" Let's also say that the directions for this research inquiry assignment require two primary sources and five secondary sources. Primary research calls us to interact with living information directly from a person, group, or place through interviews, observations, surveys, case studies, experiments, archival analysis, and service learning. This will get us into the physical spaces where these food contamination issues circulate: a visit to a local farm, a tour of the procedures for controlling crop safety, a conversation with a farmer on how food regulations affect her farming practices.

Secondary research calls us to gather other writers' research and perspectives by searching through publication modes in print and online. In this case, we can do much of our research from a computer since university libraries offer an online database, and we can also consult the library's books and reference materials. Through secondary research, you are not bound to place-based learning, but can tap into the perspectives of farmers, politicians, lawyers, consumers, nutritionists, and scientists around the world and from the past.

Mandatory GMO food labeling implies risks where there are none

Western Farm Press (Online Exclusive), 12/2011
Genetically engineered foods, Food, Biotechnology
Journal Article: Full Text Online

Figure 1 - Scholarly perspective concerning farmers and food contamination, from Kresge Library's One Search

While primary research methods are more explicitly hands-on, the idea of research writing as perspectives interacting should start with secondary research. Professors will not only expect you to remember the five articles you read for a research project, but to facilitate the conversation among the five perspectives behind those articles—in essence, creating a new text that brings these perspectives together to come to an updated conclusion. This higher critical thinking is *synthesis*, orchestrating a symphony of voices on a topic. In this chapter, we will reframe secondary research from a process of gathering information to representing multiple perspectives and evaluating what each one offers. To facilitate this process, let's continue with this research question on food production and contamination.

Sources as Contextual Perspectives Rather Than Static Information

Research analysis and synthesis start with gathering data not based merely on what pops up on the first page of your search for sources, but by seeking out important perspectives on a topic. In short, we should pay attention to *who* is writing rather than vaguely referring to "an article" saying something. This slight shift leads to deeper and more engaging research analysis: *What motivates the writer? Is she/he reacting to someone? How do these factors bolster or reduce her/his credibility?*

www.brennerlawfirm.com/pdf/food-contamination.pdf

Brenner, Ford, Monroe & Scott

FOOD CONTAMINATION CASES IN ILLINOIS
Scott R. Britton

The number of food-borne pathogens has increased five-fold since 1942. In a September 1999 study by the Centers for Disease Control (CDC), it was reported that there were 76 million reported cases of food-borne illnesses in the United States every year. Additionally, there are a reported 325,000 hospitalizations and 5,000 deaths.

People rely on the skill and care of others to catch, grow, gather, preserve, prepare and provide much of the food and drink indispensable to survival. Because pure uncontaminated food is essential for survival, most people are extraordinarily dependent for their health and safety on the care and skill of food providers. As such, the rules that govern liability for selling defective food and drink have long stood apart from those concerning other types of products.

Figure 2 - Lawyer's perspective on food contamination

Let's get to work searching for perspectives related to the question, "Would more federal regulation on plant-based food production reduce food contamination?" If we enter the terms "federal" and "food contamination" in a popular search engine, we might find a lawyer's perspective. In this example (Figure 2), Britton (n.d.) sounds knowledgeable as he cites ways food contamination cases are treated in court, but it is primarily a guide for how a victim should anticipate the process of suing a company for food contamination. He may know a lot about food contamination cases, but you wonder whether this lawyer's perspective will help you answer your question: *What perspectives are the most valuable? Which are missing from this conversation? What about a nutritionist, politician, consumer, or farmer? Who is the most knowledgeable, and who holds the most influence?* (They are often not the same person.) Just by asking these questions, you have evaluated your research in a way that makes your instructors jump for joy and, even more importantly, that applies your writing to the people and places involved in this inquiry. All of these perspectives shed light on food contamination from a different angle, offering variety to your research and paper.

When searching popular websites for academic research, we have to do extra work to find where the information comes from and whether the author is an expert or a layperson. The main motivation for the website where the lawyer's PDF came from (Figure 2) is to gain a potential client's confidence and, ultimately, gain more business. This is why secondary research requirements might call for a certain number of books, articles, or webpages. But in the digital age, deciding which sources are the best for your project can be tricky since information often looks the same and there are no longer restrictions on who can publish their writing. Therefore, let's simplify this by researching *perspectives* rather than *information* in general: Know who wrote the article—name, credentials, motivation, ideology—and what their perspective contributes to your inquiry. Through this single task, you will add more life, authority, and insight to your academic writing.

Traditional Approach to Research

What are the first three synonyms for "sources" that pop up in your mind?

Maybe "books," "articles," "information"? Usually these are the types of publications we're most familiar with because we start our research careers with this definition of sources. This makes sense since these are the written forms in which information comes to us, but here's the problem: If we just think of books, articles, and information as sources, we forget that there are people's voices behind them. And if we aren't thinking of the people who wrote the information, we likely aren't thinking of the larger context that caused their texts to come to us in a print or online form. *Who is the audience? What kairotic element brought this piece of writing into existence? What is the writer's motivation and goal?* The Western Farm Press (Figure 1) is more likely to produce scholarship that is skeptical of too much food regulation because the journal's perspective comes from farmers who earn their living from plant production.

To help us consider how to search for perspectives and use the research we find, Cynthia Haller (2011), an associate professor of English at CUNY York, uses a helpful metaphor for how to use research—walking, talking, cooking, and eating. The *talking* part forces us to consider who is having a conversation on the topic at hand: Haller observes that "It helps us to know who the authors are. What they're saying. When, where, and to whom they're saying it. And what their purposes are" (p. 201). This is where the *rhetoric of*

OU's Writing and Rhetoric classes comes into play. In order to understand and evaluate what someone writes, we have to know the larger context implied by their words on the page. So let's go beyond defining sources as "[b]ooks and articles" to "'forms of meaning you use to make meaning,'" (Haller, 2011, p. 194), which forces us to consider how that meaning was packaged and how we will repurpose it in our writing.

Prewriting: Mapping How Perspectives Interact

Before beginning research, consider what relevant perspectives you will need in order to answer your inquiry question or complete your project. Start with listing all of the related perspectives you can think of, and then pare this down to the perspectives that are most important to your inquiry. If you want to focus on only a couple of perspectives, make it clear that you are excluding other perspectives purposefully.

Once you have picked a few perspectives, map out how you expect these perspectives will interact by characterizing their relationships to one another:

- Whose interests are directly opposed to one another?

- Whose interests are similar to one another?

- Who presents the possibility of compromise?

Is the relationship . . .

- antagonistic?

- supportive?

- unrelated?

- directly related to success?

- directly related to failure?

- part of the other?

- dependent on the other?

Let's see what this could look like working with the inquiry we have used so far:

Would more federal regulation on plant-based food production reduce food contamination?

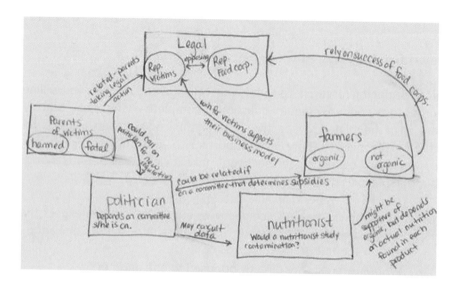

Figure 3 - Mapping relevant perspectives

This example maps five perspectives (some with divided perspectives, circled) by considering how their interests clash or coalesce: *Is a nutritionist the best scholarly perspective to consider on contamination? Do politicians who align themselves with big food corporations risk acting against the interest of their constituents' health?* This map helps prepare us not only to search for a certain perspective, but also tells us what to look for in this perspective. Since we already have begun considering the interest of each perspective, we are primed for critical reading of the perspectives we find in research.

Categorizing Authority

Perhaps this next exercise should be published in pop-up book form (there really should be more of those in textbooks and academic journals), but let's start with a little exercise:

What kind of people write . . .

a. academic journal articles? _____

b. newspaper articles? _____

c. blog entries? _____

Really, take a moment to answer these three questions.

Reproductive Health And The Industrialized Food System: A Point Of Intervention For Health Policy
Sutton, Patrice; Wallinga, David; Perron, Joanne; Gottlieb, Michelle; Sayre, Lucia; Woodruff, Tracey
Health Affairs; May 2011; 30, 5; ProQuest Business Collection
pg. 888

Citation information offered

Digital object identifier, journal name

REGULATING CHEMICAL USE

DOI: 10.1377/hlthaff.2010.1255
HEALTH AFFAIRS 30,
NO. 5 (2011): 888-897
©2011 Project HOPE—
The People-to-People Health
Foundation, Inc.

By Patrice Sutton, David Wallinga, Joanne Perron, Michelle Gottlieb, Lucia Sayre, and Tracey Woodruff

Reproductive Health And The Industrialized Food System: A Point Of Intervention For Health Policy

Multiple authors with expert perspectives

Patrice Sutton (suttonp@ obgyn.ucsf.edu) is a research scientist at the Program on Reproductive Health and the Environment, at the University of California, in Oakland, California.

David Wallinga is director of the Food and Health Institute for Agriculture and Trade Policy, in Minneapolis, Minnesota.

Joanne Perron is a post doctoral fellow at the Program on Reproductive Health and the Environment.

Michelle Gottlieb is codirector of Food Systems Health Care Without Harm, in Reston, Virginia.

Lucia Sayre is codirector of the San Francisco Bay Area Physicians for Social Responsibility, in Berkeley, California.

ABSTRACT What food is produced, and how, can have a critical impact on human nutrition and the environment, which in turn are key drivers of healthy human reproduction and development. The US food production system yields a large volume of food that is relatively low in cost for consumers but is often high in calories and low in nutritional value. In this article we examine the evidence that intensive use of pesticides, chemical fertilizers, hormones, antibiotics, and fossil fuel in food production, as well as chemicals in food packaging, are potentially harmful to human reproductive and developmental health. We conclude that policies to advance a healthy food system are necessary to prevent adverse reproductive health effects and avoid associated health costs among current and future generations. These policies include changes to the Farm Bill and the Toxic Substances Control Act, and greater involvement by the health care sector in supporting and sourcing food from urban agriculture programs, farmers' markets, and local food outlets, as well as increasing understanding by clinicians of the links between reproductive health and industrialized food production.

Figure 4 - Evaluating an academic journal article

Now that you have answered the questions, let's pull back the figurative pop-up flaps for the answers: The majority of the time, university professors and researchers write for journals, journalists write for newspapers, and laypeople write blogs (a bit trickier and not as consistent, but more on that later). This is why we have learned that authority falls into certain types of publications: journal articles and books published by university presses are more authoritative because they require a rigorous review process. Scholars write them for other scholars to read, which is why they don't have to look attractive like a magazine. So how are these articles different from newspapers, which also offer a lot of information and are not as attractive as a glossy copy of *Cosmopolitan*? Since newspapers serve a wider public audience, they are shorter and less complicated. And let's get into the habit of considering the voice behind the publication. Journalists are smart people, but they are skilled at writing on a variety of topics and gathering primary research for short-term projects. Since scholars study large, specialized projects for years, they have more authority on any single topic than journalists. Consider the complete process behind each publication. For a typical journal article, a scholar may spend six months researching and writing; then, after months of peer review and revision, the paper is accepted for publication. On the other hand, a newspaper or magazine journalist might go through this whole process anywhere from a few days to a few weeks.

Since academic journals are written for an audience of scholars, Google does not have as wide of access to these journals as university libraries. As an Oakland University student engaging in this world of academic research, you have access to hundreds of journals through Kresge Library. Library search engines can filter the type of publications in our search results. When we do not need newspaper articles, we can exclude them from our search. Sources are also listed with the researcher in mind, offering a clear explanation for what kind of publication and perspective each source offers.

University libraries will not include popular webpages since they are less stable and established. A blog, for example, may be published without any editorial board approval or publication filter: anyone can make a blog. Digital media is now so accessible that students use them to publish writing for school projects—sometimes as early as elementary school. When using our same food contamination search terms on Google, "Federal Food Regulation Reforms are Needed" comes up from the blog "Alleged Students" (Loucks, 2012). The "About This Blog" information reveals that students authored this blog as part of a college class. This is where understanding the author helps: with online sources, you have to work a little harder to understand the authority of writers and their published work. Scholars, journalists, and students can write blogs, so it is up to you to learn more about the person writing the blog. You may find that certain blogs offer an important perspective to your paper. For example, if you are writing about citizens organizing a class-action lawsuit related to food contamination, and Average Joe hosts the blog through which hundreds of these victims communicate, then his perspective might be worth including.

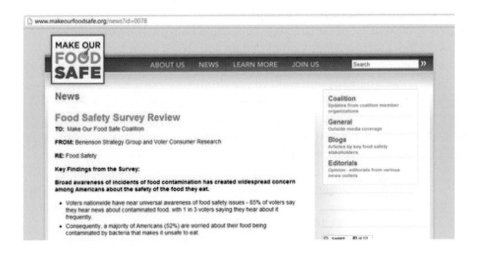

Figure 5 - Make Our Food Safe, an organization of victim consumers found through popular media

Based on these examples, we should understand that searching popular and non-academic media is not "bad" and always unnecessary for an academic project. Popular media can provide a current, localized, everyday perspective an academic journal may not capture. For this food contamination inquiry, gathering perspectives from consumers, victims, and activist organizations from blogs may build your *ethos* and inject *pathos* into your writing. News-papers may offer the most current food contamination cases. Partnering the current, widespread nature of popular sources with scholarly, in-depth stud-ies can work very well to bring a number of valuable perspectives to your research. The trouble arises when we treat data reported in *The Huffington Post* as if it were published in *British Medical Journal* (BMJ). Understanding the perspective of each source we include prevents this issue, and helps us see the larger picture: scholars publish ground-breaking data, and journalists use popular media to transmit the most important findings to the public.

Steps for Researching and Writing with Perspectives

Now that we have gone through the *whys* and *hows* of using perspectives to guide your research, let's boil it down to an action plan.

1. **Plan Perspectives to Include**
   Write a list of perspectives that could help answer your question. Picture what kind of people you would want to talk with in order to get a well-rounded, informed answer. Articulate in writing what you want to gain from each perspective: For example, you would include a lawyer's perspective for a legal perspective and a doctor for a medical perspective (see Figure 3 for a visual map of this writing process.) This seems obvious, but when you begin your research, you may be tempted to cite medical information from a law firm's website, which could decrease your *ethos* and misrepresent medical facts.

2. **Inquire Where to Find Those Perspectives**
   After searching on your own and consulting a librarian, decide where to look for these perspectives. If you want a teacher's perspective, get in contact with teachers in your local area and ask them where to look. If you need a nutritionist's perspective, search scholarly journals that specialize in nutrition. Digital support systems are often found in blogs and forums—even social media networks like Facebook and Twitter can be fruitful for a public, popular perspective.

3. **Search the Name**
   While scholarly journal articles offer a short biography of an author (see Figure 4), many publications will only offer an author's name. So, how do you find out exactly what perspective an author offers?

   - Seek biographical information in a scholarly journal or at the beginning of a book.

   - If you know an author is a professor at a specific institution, look for that professor's faculty page on the university's department website.

   - Since websites often have "About" pages, look there for more information on the author. Web articles often hyperlink an author's name to more information about the author or more of the author's writing.

○ Plug the name into a search engine.

If a name is not included with the information, then move onto a more reliable source; "Knowing which texts you can trust means understanding which authors you can trust" (Haller, 2011, p. 201). Academic writing holds a high standard of credibility, so you don't need to waste your time with nameless information.

4. **Refine and Synthesize Perspectives**
   Revisit and revise the perspectives you mapped (Figure 3), and decide which ones to develop into a well-informed answer to an inquiry. This will help you decide which perspectives, from the ones you have collected in research, are the most informative, relevant, interesting, and overall useful to your project.

5. **Include Appositives in Your Writing**
   As you revise your papers, a quick way to solidify your perspectives and check to make sure you have included all of the perspectives you wanted is to add an *appositive* to the authors you introduce. Provide a short phrase that allows your readers to understand the information you introduce (example: "Mark T. Law, *associate professor of economics at University of Vermont,* says . . ."). While appositives are short, easy, and helpful to the reader, write them in a way that best communicates their authority and relevance to your academic project.

This shift in researching for perspectives is the foundation for more interesting writing to come. From here you can synthesize your information by writing two paragraphs on how all of your perspectives respond to one subtopic, or several paragraphs on how these perspectives would approach a problem. *What foods do farmers, nutritionists, and consumers consider the most improperly regulated? How do these perspectives comment on the role of federal regulation?* Here lies the gap that often separates the writing a student offers and an instructor's expectations. A student might report numerous facts from the five different sources specified in the requirements, when the teacher really wants the student to go further and show why these sources are worth including and evaluating.

As you hit the books and browse websites, rather than looking for *sources*, dig for *perspectives* and a better understanding of the people who share them and the best way to evaluate their data.

Exercises

1. As shown in Figure 3, draw a perspectives map: pick one of the inquiry questions below, list perspectives that would help you answer the question, pick 3-5 of the most relevant ones, and map out the relationship between those perspectives using the bullets in the "Prewriting" section. *If you are working with your own inquiry, map it instead.*

   a. Should college campuses provide gender-neutral bathrooms?

   b. How do students determine whether they should commute to a local campus or live on campus?

   c. What elements make up the most successful commercial Facebook pages?

   d. How can we calculate the ecological footprint of exotic produce?

   e. Should high schools equip each of their students with iPads in lieu of textbooks?

   f. What are the top five lifestyle changes every adult should make to ward off cancer?

2. What perspectives might you exclude from the inquiry topic chosen in No. 1? Why?

References

Britton, S. R. (n.d.) Food contamination cases in Illinois. Retrieved from http://www.brennerlawfirm.com/pdf/food-contamination.pdf

Haller, C. (2011). Walk, talk, cook, eat: A guide to using sources. *Writing spaces: Readings on writing, 2.* Retrieved from http://writingspaces.org/essays.

Louks, C. (2012, September 4). Federal food regulation reforms are needed. [Web log comment]. Retrieved from http://allegedstudents.wordpress.com/2012/09/04/federal-food-regulation-reforms-are-needed/

[14]

SYNTHESIS:
Fusing Sources to Create Something New

Marilyn Borner

In first year writing (FYW) courses, you may be called upon to "synthesize" sources. The ability to synthesize begins with your own curiosity about a topic. Using critical thinking and research skills, you must figure out how to add to an ongoing discussion in the field. Researching what has already been written on a topic, knowing what has already been said, is an obvious first step toward synthesizing a discussion.

Synthesis Defined

Synthesis in its most basic form is weaving together information found in several sources in order to generate new ideas. It is a bringing together of shared concepts. Synthesis begins with your own curiosity. As you begin to research a particular topic, you interpret, analyze, and evaluate what has already been said. Once you have a clear understanding of the topic, you can then elucidate, illustrate, or intimate a concept in greater detail for your audience, adding your own new commentary on the topic, thus adding to the conversation.

You may be asked to synthesize when crafting an argument, comparing and contrasting two or more ideas or concepts, or showing cause and effect. Synthesis is, according to Spivey, "a common academic task requiring students to *select, organize,* and *connect* content from source texts as they compose their own new texts" (as cited in Segev-Miller, 2004, p. 5).

The basic idea behind synthesis is to help your readers more fully understand a subject by guiding them through a variety of texts and offering your own commentary as a result of that combined information. As blogger Karncha-noke (2010) puts it, synthesis entails:

- Analyzing and making sense of the texts for your reader;

- Assessing the validity of the texts;

- Reorganizing ideas from the texts;

- Selecting and including only relevant parts from the texts;

- Pointing out the relationship among ideas in the texts; and

- Pointing out the relationship between ideas from the texts and your own ideas. (What Is Synthesizing section, para. 1)

Synthesis at its best is not simply learning to write, it's writing to learn. Ideally, you will select your own topic for research, something that you feel driven to learn more about.

Reasons for Synthesis

We synthesize sources in order to make a contribution to the ongoing dia-logue within any given field. According to Flower (1989), academic discourse "places special value on integrating one's own ideas and knowledge into the written conversation with one's sources" (p. 26). An important part of aca-demic life is the sharing of knowledge. You learn from your instructors, of course, but you also learn from other writers and your peers as well.

Most of the time you will be asked to synthesize for a particular reason, per-haps a written report, an oral history, an essay or a research paper. In your professional life, you may also be called upon to synthesize, for example, when your boss asks you to evaluate two or more proposals and make a rec-ommendation about which way to proceed. Police at the scene of an acci-dent gather and synthesize information from multiple sources. They interview the people involved in the accident, collect witnesses' accounts, and compile data and evidence found at the scene to produce an accurate report of the incident. Synthesis occurs across multiple platforms and in every discourse community. It's a handy skill to learn and not just because it will help you in your first-year writing courses here.

A Working Synthesis

When preparing to synthesize, your curiosity leads you toward research, which then gives you a basis on which to formulate new ideas and opinions on a particular topic. You may review what's been written about the topic to glean a more complete idea of what others have said and how you can add to the discussion.

Caution: Don't begin your research with an opinion and then seek out only sources that support it. Rather, you should begin with curiosity and read everything you can on the topic before entering the conversation. Beginning your research with an opinion will often lead to a paper that is just a rehash of what others have said.

Let's say you've just spent $5,300 for tuition for all of your classes this semester. You think this amount seems outrageous. You're curious about why tuition costs so much and wonder if there's anything that can be done to solve this growing problem. You question whether there has been anything written about the topic of the rising costs of tuition in recent years and how those rising costs impact society.

This is where research begins. You begin by creating a question to guide your research: "Why are tuition prices so high and what can be done about these prices?" Once you have a clear question or questions in mind to guide your research, you can then consult sources and glean from them everything you need to enter the conversation.

Gathering the information you need from your sources can be challenging, as Perin, Keselman, and Monopoli (2003) suggest, "when consulting informational text, the writer needs to understand the content, search the text for specific information, extract the gist, label certain information as important, integrate identified information with previous knowledge, connect information across sources, and organize the information" (p. 20).

At the library, after a thorough investigation of the topic, you find several sources that address the issue. Now it's time to analyze and interpret what you've found and then enter the conversation. Some methods for interacting with the sources you've found might include the following:

- Think about the source material you've just read. Did you find it useful? Why or why not?

- Write down your own brief impressions of the source. What type of a source was it—book, newspaper article, journal article, YouTube video, radio spot, TV program, etc.? What was the basic premise of the piece? Did you agree with it? Why or why not?

- Evaluate the source. Is it reliable? How do you know? Is there any bias in the work?

- Consider the author. What do you know about this person or group? What purpose did the author have in constructing this text? Who was the target audience?

- Consider the structure. How is this piece organized? Why do you think the author chose that method of organization?

- Analyze the material. Has the author used formal or informal language? What tone does the author convey? Has the author used any literary techniques such as similes, metaphors, analogies, personification, etc.? What purpose do they serve?

- Ponder the implications. Has this text raised any questions in your own mind about the topic? Does it reveal a side of the topic you hadn't considered before? How does it fit with what you already knew about the topic? Did it cause you to change your mind about the topic?

Next, you will want to analyze your sources to determine how they are similar or different in their approach to the topic. You may want to create a diagram illustrating which points your sources seem to agree on and which points they disagree on. Once you understand how the various sources you're consulting might talk to one another about your topic, you'll be in a better position to draw conclusions or generalizations about your topic and to synthesize what you've learned for your readers.

When you finally sit down to write your synthesis, you will want to create a thesis statement, and then form opinions based on your analysis of what you've read. Let the material you've considered become material that you can use to comment on. This is where your research really becomes exciting. After researching the topic, several ideas will begin to emerge. You may see patterns within the texts, similarities, differences, themes, or facts and figures that are repeated in different sources. As you find connections between sources, you'll start to get a feeling for the overall ongoing conversation about your topic. You'll also see how your views and stance may speak to others, and you'll offer your own ideas on the topic, as one Oakland University student did in the passage below:

> College tuition has been rising at a higher rate than inflation for years now. It has caused many students and families to struggle to afford college for one child, let alone two or three. The amount of debt most students incur is hurting American society.

As you continue your conversation, you might consider what the reader will want to know about the causes of tuition hikes. Remembering that you read something about this, you return to your sources as this OU student did here:

> Even though "state and local financing of public colleges, across the board, has grown, so has the number of students at public colleges. As a result, per-student spending actually declined by nearly 8 percent in the five years after 2002" (Blumenstyk, 2008, Straining students section, para. 6). The result of this lack of revenue almost always results in tuition increases in order to compensate.

Here, you may recall a few statistics or facts that you've read that would elucidate the problem. This would probably be a good place to comment on what you've read. Our student continued:

> Due to these increases in tuition and university costs, "the cost of college has more than doubled since 2000, outpacing the rate of inflation...and college loan debt is now greater than the national cumulative credit card debt" (McCullough, 2011, p. 1). This is especially true of those who are below middle class. According to a National Center for Public Policy and Higher Education report, "The cost of tuition, room, and board at a four-year public college, even after taking into account financial aid, was equivalent to 55 percent of the household income

of the poorest 10 percent of American families in 2007, compared with 39 percent in 2000" (Blumenstyk, 2008, para. 7).

You will want to remember that the purpose of synthesis is to bring new ideas and meaning to the issue at hand, thus entering the conversation by adding your own commentary, as our student did:

> If these trends in tuition continue, more than just the poor will be affected. Soon we will price ourselves right out of a college degree and a large amount of us will be unable to even dream of higher education due to its immense expense.

Synthesis is not just a method of dropping supporting quotes into a text without contextualizing them. Synthesis is not a string of outside source materials and citations. It is also not just a paraphrase of what you have read. McGregor (2011) argues that, "the idea of synthesizing means creating something new (even if at the most basic level it is simply new to the writer), and that requires more than replacing words with synonyms" (para. 2). Synthesis also isn't a way to avoid critically thinking about the issue by simply restating what others have said.

Source Citation

One of the most important elements of synthesis is to be able to integrate source material into your writing, giving credit where credit is due. Using whatever style guide your instructor recommends, credit any ideas and direct quotes to the source in which they appeared. It's not enough just to credit direct quotes, though. *Any* idea that isn't your original thought, even if you've only summarized it or paraphrased it, needs attribution in the form of both an in-text (parenthetical) citation and a listing on your Works Cited, References, or similar bibliographic page.

You will have noticed that the example above synthesizes three sources, and each source is either introduced with a signal phrase identifying the author and/ or ends with a parenthetical citation. Your readers should clearly be able to determine where your quote, paraphrase or summary begins and ends. In other words, your reader should have no trouble identifying what parts of your paragraph came from outside sources and what parts came from your own ideas.

When including material from several sources to support the point that you are making, it is also inadvisable to run two or more quotes back to back in your text. Instead, you should write around the quoted material, adding your commentary and including your voice to the paragraph. The reader wants to hear your own voice, not just the voices of your sources. So you should always remember that the ultimate goal is for you to enter the conversation.

Synthesis Revision

Revision and self-reflection is an important final step for writing any essay. When you revise, be sure that all outside source material is cited and that the reader can clearly identify where each idea from an outside source begins and ends. Remember that the reader is interested in hearing your opinions and thoughts, so it should be clear in your text where each author is speaking and where you are speaking. The majority of your source synthesis should be the new ideas that you want to contribute to the established conversation. Finally, you should always be on the lookout for places in your text where you may have used too much outside material and not enough of your own commentary.

Exercise

1. Interview three or four students in your class or your dorm about their experiences in purchasing textbooks for this semester. Synthesize what they've told you in order to draw some conclusions about the cost of textbooks and the best ways and places to purchase them.

References

Blumenstyk, G. (2008). The $375-billion question: Why does college cost so much? *The Chronicle of Higher Education*, 55(6). Retrieved from http://chronicle.com/article/The-375-Billion-Question-Why/26459/

Flower, L. (1989). Negotiating academic discourse (Reading-to-Write Report No. 29). *The Center for the Study of Writing*, Pittsburgh, Pennsylvania/ Berkeley, California.

Karnchanoke. (2010). Organizing and synthesizing [Weblog]. *EFL writing for life*. Retrieved from http://eflwriting4life.wordpress.com/2010/10/24/synthesizing-information/

McCullough, A. (2011). The college bubble: Many students believe some majors (or degree programs) aren't worth the debt that must be taken on to pay tuition. *Mississippi Business Journal*, 33(47), 1-3.

McGregor, J. (2011). A visual approach: Teaching synthesis. *School Library Monthly*, 27(8). Retrieved from http://www.schoollibrarymonthly.com/articles/Mcgregor2011-v27n8p5.html

Perin, D., Keselman, A., & Monopoli, M. (2003). The academic writing of community college remedial students: Text and learner variables. *Higher Education*, 45, 19-42. http://www.jstor.org/stable/3447512

Segev-Miller, R. (2004). Writing from sources: The effect of explicit instruction on college students' processes and products. *L1-Educational Studies in Language and Literature*, 4(1), 5-33. Retrieved from http://www.springerlink.com/content/wk6t602h2474rl1k/

[15]

CONSTRUCTING A SOLID PIECE OF WRITING:
Peer Review and Collaboration

Lauren E. Rinke

If you go to work on your goals, your goals will go to work on you. If you go to work on your plan, your plan will go to work on you. Whatever good things we build end up building us.

> – Jim Rohn, entrepreneur and
> business philosopher

Good design begins with honesty, asks tough questions, and comes from collaboration and from trusting your intuition.

> – Freeman Thomas, automotive designer

Overview

This chapter will illustrate how peer review will benefit your development as both a writer and a student. Working with your classmates in collaborative editing will lead to recognizing your strengths and weaknesses as a writer, enhancing your critical reading skills, creating a sense of comfort and community within your writing class, and assisting you in creating your best work possible: texts that are equally coherent and engaging. Peer review sessions are essential to composing a variety of texts: from written essays to visual arguments and multimodal presentations.

Building a Foundation

Imagine that you've been asked to build your own home. You know what makes a strong house: wood, nails, bricks, mortar, a solid foundation, and a water-resistant roof. You've laid out the plans in your mind, sketched a design complete with measurements, and you're ready to build the finished product. There's just one problem—you know you can't build the house alone. It would be virtually impossible, so you call some of your friends to help. Your friends are there when you need them, so naturally they show up, take a look at your plans, and you begin to build the home together. Assuming your design to be nearly perfect, you are taken aback when one of your friends has noticed a flaw in the drawing of the home's foundation. Of course, you don't want your house to crumble or falter under the elements, so you listen to what your friend has to say. You realize you've overlooked an important element in your building strategy, so you take your friend's suggestion and continue building with a new-and-improved architectural plan. Another friend shares an idea regarding the aesthetics of the layout. She is under the impression that the downstairs bathroom should be moved to a different location. Even though you value this friend's opinion, you feel that your original choice is the most visually appealing and lends to the overall flow of the house. You decide not to take her advice, and move forward with the building process.

As with any major undertaking, it is always important to consider the feedback of others. As the old saying goes, "No one is an island." Endeavors that require much effort and time also necessitate multiple sets of eyes, ears, and a variety of opinions. Just as you would likely consider many opinions if you were building a home, you should also regard the feedback of other student writers when composing an essay. Of course, a piece of writing ultimately belongs to you—you are the author. Writing is an extension of the self, and what we write can be very personal and private. But you must remember, too, you will always be composing your ideas to be read by a specific audience. Your primary goal is to effectively communicate your ideas to those readers, and peer review sessions will help you do just that.

What Is Peer Review?

Coming into your first semester at Oakland University, you may already have some experience with peer review. Perhaps one of your high school English teachers required you to work with classmates in revising an essay, or maybe you've only heard of peer review. Regardless of your previous experience, you should know that your WRT 102, WRT 150 and WRT 160 instructors will ask you to participate in some form of collaborative review. You may already have an understanding of what peer review is, but let's spell it out so we're all on the same page. At OU, we call this important process "peer review," but you also may have heard the terms "peer revision," "peer editing," "peer workshop," etc. There are many forms of peer review, but all of these terms essentially mean the same thing: you'll be working with one or more of your classmates to review your writing.

Writing is a process, and your instructors will likely break down major assignments into steps, including prewriting and drafting. You will be asked to prepare a draft of your paper before the final draft is due, so that your peer review partner or group can respond to your writing, address the structure of your essay, and let you know if they think you've fulfilled the requirements for the assignment. You will be responsible for peer reviewing your classmates' writing as well.

In your first-year writing classes, you will encounter a variety of peer review settings, chosen by your instructor to best fit the type of assignment you're working on. If you have a fully or partially online class, your instructor may require you to participate in an online peer review session. For our traditional sections of first-year writing, you may be asked to take part in a face-to-face peer review session with one or more classmates. Regardless of the review location or requirements, it's essential to focus on the larger issues you see in your peers' drafts, rather than on small issues with grammar, punctuation or spelling—but we'll come back to that later.

What Makes a "Rough" Draft?

So, you have an idea of the context in which you might find peer review, and where you might participate in this collaborative activity, but let's also explore the stage in writing we call a "rough draft." You know you'll be required to complete a rough draft for peer review, but what constitutes a "rough" draft exactly? Let's go back to our building metaphor for a moment. Before you can begin the actual building of a home, you need to have the plans sketched out, which is a lot like prewriting. Your instructor may ask you to create some sort of outline or idea map, to get a feel for the way you'd like your main topics to flow in your essay. The next step in building a home is laying out the foundation and framework, onto which you'll base the finished product (dry-wall, siding, etc.). The elements involved in creating the finished product cannot be included until the entire foundation and frame are completed and inspected by an expert.

Think of your rough draft in this way: the draft is essentially a complete version of the essay, but it may still need alterations in big things like organization, argument, and support. Coming to class unprepared on peer review days or uploading only a few pages of a 6-8-page essay will not give your peer reviewers a complete framework ready for their inspection. You would not ask a home inspector to review only a partial frame or foundation. The more you have completed going into the peer review session, the better your feedback on your paper is going to be.

Effective Communication: Having Your Work Reviewed

Preparation is an essential element for a successful peer review session. Equally important is the ability to effectively communicate with your partner or group. Maybe you're outgoing or maybe you're shy. Either way, you're going to be asked to share your writing and have a conversation about it. As previously mentioned, writing can be very personal and sometimes difficult to share. But keep this in mind, even your instructors are asked to share their writing, and peer review is an essential part of all academic work. A journal article cannot be published until several academics have the chance to review the writing and research. Even this chapter had to be peer reviewed and edited many times before going to press. Likewise, research studies published in medical journals must go through a rigorous review process to ensure that the work written is accurate. In the medical community, writers take peer review seriously because just one error in accuracy or clarity could mean life or death for sick patients.

It's not very likely that your writing will have life or death implications, but you will come to realize how important it is for you to trust in the peer review process. Your classmates are in the same position as you, and they probably feel just as nervous about sharing their writing as you do. Remember that you are working to help each other improve. Sharing your writing and reading others' writing will help you recognize both your strengths and weaknesses. So, take a deep breath and hand over that draft. Your group or partner will probably surprise you with the quality of their feedback.

Okay, you've gotten past the first hard part: sharing your writing. Now what? How will your group know what to look for, what to comment on, or what kind of feedback to give? Here's a simple answer: have a conversation. Your instructor may give you a set of questions to address while reviewing, but there are four main points you should cover before reading each other's essays:

1. What are your expectations going into this peer review session? What do you hope to get out of it?

2. What are your strengths as a writer? What do you struggle with the most? What do you want your partner(s) to keep an eye out for?

3. What was your approach when writing this essay? What were your goals? What were the main points you were trying to communicate?

4. Who is your intended audience? Why do you want them to read this piece of writing? Are you trying to inform or persuade your audience?

Don't be afraid to ask your peer for specific feedback. You should lead the discussion in order to get the responses and constructive criticism you're looking for. In addition, listen carefully to any questions your peer reviewer has before reading your essay, and try to answer their questions about your draft as completely as you can.

Giving Criticism: Reviewing Your Peers' Work

When it's time for you to respond to your peers' work, they will probably give you an overview of the main goals and concerns they have about their work. Be sure to listen carefully and take notes so that you can give the best feedback possible. You may be nervous entering into this role as reviewer, or wonder how you'll offer any advice, being a novice writer yourself. But keep this in mind: after reading this chapter, receiving help from your instructor and having a conversation with your peers, you'll be poised to offer some really helpful and constructive criticism. The suggestions you give your classmate(s) will be integral to their creating a polished piece of writing and to their success communicating their ideas.

Make sure you ask questions if something is unclear in your peers' papers, both before and during the review process. Sometimes, honest reactions are just as helpful as specific feedback. However, it's important that you always remain respectful of your peers while reviewing their work. If, in your mind, you find yourself thinking, *"This makes no sense!"* or *"What does this have to do with anything?"* try to rephrase your thoughts before asking the writer those questions. For example, ask your peer to read the section that seems unclear, and see if s/he can explain it in his or her own words. Again, it's okay to have an honest reaction to a piece of writing (whether positive or negative), and to give the writer a sense of how his/her readers may respond, but take a moment to think about how you can reword your thoughts to create a constructive conversation. Remember, writing is personal, and you don't want to end up offending your partner with harsh language or emotional reactions to the writing.

Avoiding Universal Praise and Personal Comments

One of the hardest parts of a successful peer review session is offering feedback that is both respectful and helpful. There are several different kinds of criticism, and certain kinds are more helpful than others. It's tempting to want to give positive responses to writing like, "It's good" or "I like it" without offering any specific reasons for these observations. Yes, it's important to let your classmate know that you like the essay or that it is successful in meeting the assignment requirements, but generalized statements of universal praise offer no constructive reasoning for your reactions. You should add specific examples to your responses so that your peer will know how to move forward. For example, you might say: "The essay is good because the argument is clear and you gave a good variety of scholarly support and statistics to prove your point" or "I really like your essay because it engages me as a reader. The example you gave in the second paragraph made me interested in reading further and it really showed me why this is an important issue." Calling attention to specific strengths or areas for improvement will add value to your more generalized reactions.

In addition, it's important to avoid personal comments, which reflect on personality traits or the individual, rather than the writing. For example, if you see a theme of darkness or sadness in the essay you're reviewing, it may be tempting to respond by saying, "You don't know what you're talking about." or "Your writing makes me sad." Again, feedback of this sort is not really helpful. However, that doesn't mean that emotional reactions can't be turned into productivity. Consider rewording emotional statements that criticize the individual, into feedback that focuses on the writing. For example, you might say "I noticed a theme of darkness in your writing that might distract the reader from your main points" or "some of the language used in your essay seems a little biased. You may want to consider rewording these areas to make sure this language doesn't hurt your ethos." Your emotional reactions can be beneficial to the writer, but only if they focus on the writing, not the writer.

Constructive Feedback: Focusing on the Text

As the previous examples show, giving your peer review partner suggestions directly from his/her essay will show them where they can revise and improve on specific areas. In addition to rephrasing universal praise and personal comments to be more productive, there are several other kinds of text-based responses, which will illustrate how your partner should move forward with his/her revisions.

Sometimes, when reviewing a classmate's writing, it can be easy to get caught up on grammar or spelling issues. "Local issues," as we call them, are important factors in creating a successful essay, but it's important not to waste time focusing on such errors early on. Calling attention to small errors in punctuation or grammar should only be done at the very end of the writing process, when the writer is polishing the final draft for submission or publication. At the end of the writing process, circling or highlighting grammar or spelling errors will call attention to the problems, so that the writer can fix them before submitting the work.

There may be issues relating to grammar, however, that will require more commentary or time on your part during the beginning stages of the review process. The writer's word choice can either add to or detract from the essay's main points or goal for communication. Concerns such as these might fall under the "Global Issues" category: problems in the writing that can detract from effective communication. Awkward or confusing areas of the essay are things you should make specific reference to. These kinds of comments reflect on the reader's needs, reactions, and understanding of the text.

Your peer review partner likely has a specific audience in mind, so it's important for you to keep that in mind while reviewing the essay. Effectively communicating to one's audience is a major aspect of a successful essay. If you see any areas that need rephrasing or reworking because you think they could confuse or mislead the reader, make specific reference to those areas in the text. In your comments, make note of how you think the reader might misperceive these passages, as well. You might write, for example, "Your word choice here is a little confusing. The reader might think you are for lowering the drinking age, but according to your thesis and introduction, the paper illustrates why the drinking age should remain at 21. Rephrase this section so that it accurately reflects your argument." Similarly, repetitive phrases should be noted, as the reader may become disinterested if the writing is not sufficiently engaging.

There are several other global issues, which can interfere with effective communication. One of the biggest culprits in confusing one's reader is essay structure/organization. Although your instructor will likely illustrate the importance of pre-writing strategies, it can oftentimes be difficult to organize ideas into coherent paragraphs early in the writing process. Pay attention to the way your peer's text is structured, and be sure the organization makes sense in terms of the writer's audience and purpose. If you find yourself questioning the order of ideas, make a note of it. It may be a matter of simply reorganizing the paragraphs, or combining ideas that seem to be repeated. Notes on structure work best as margin comments, where the writer can make a direct connection between the place in the text where there is an organizational issue and your suggestion for change.

Another important global issue to watch out for is the writer's tone and voice. Go back to the conversation you shared with your partner about his/her goals in writing and intended audience. If you were building a house for someone, the way you would lay out the home would depend on your customer. If a single person wanted to see one of your designs, you might create a sketch for a smaller home, compared to a layout for a six-person family. Make sure the words chosen by your partner match his/her intended audience. When it comes to giving feedback on tone, it's acceptable to make comments about the overall "feel" of the voice, but even more effective is drawing the writer's attention to specific areas, which seem to lapse in the consistency of voice or audience awareness. Is the tone too casual for the intended audience? Does the writer, perhaps mistakenly, assume that the audience already has a certain amount of knowledge? Do key terms need to be clearly defined for the reader? Put yourself in the position of the intended audience, and make note of any passages that might confuse readers or that might need to be reworded.

Your instructor will likely assign you specific guidelines for peer review sessions. In addition to reading your partner's paper and offering text-based responses, you will generally be required to answer questions relating to the assignment guidelines.

The Next Step: Making Changes to Your Draft

Keep in mind that the suggestions your peer or group members make are just that—suggestions. You are the managing editor of your work, so the final decision is up to you. However, it's always important to reflect on the reasons behind your ultimate decisions. While reviewing your partners' feedback, take a moment or two to think about whether you'll incorporate their comments, and why you've made each decision. How will each suggestion benefit your finished product?

Sometimes, your instructor will offer time in class, or a space online, in which you can discuss feedback with your peer review partners. Conferencing with your classmates will allow you the opportunity to receive the clarification you need to move forward in your revisions. Don't be afraid to ask your peer review partner(s) questions regarding their comments. If something seems unclear or you don't immediately agree with the feedback, be sure to get clarification before dismissing their comments. Just as conversation plays a big part in the peer review session, communicating with your classmates during the revision process is just as important. If you're assigned to the same group or partner for the entire semester, be sure your classmates know which comments were the most beneficial to you. Open lines of communication will allow you to receive the feedback that best fits your writing needs.

Working successfully with your peers to review one another's writing will help you to improve in the areas of effective communication, collaboration and critical reading. Use peer review sessions to your advantage; every opportunity you have to share your writing is a chance to gain both skills and confidence as a writer.

Questions for Further Discussion

1. Identify some of your strengths and weaknesses as a writer. How can you use both the positives and negatives to offer constructive peer response?

2. What was your perception of peer review before reading this chapter? How do you feel you can use this information to benefit you in your first-year writing classes?

3. Discuss the difference between "global" and "local" issues, and how to provide feedback in both areas. What are some global issues you should be on the lookout for during the peer review for your next paper?

4. Look at comments your instructor has made on previous as-signments. How can they be modeled or used in peer review sessions? Which comments are the most beneficial to you as a writer? Why were those comments beneficial to you?

5. Take the peer review pledge!

   I know that sharing my writing will improve my writing. I vow to remain open to constructive criticism, ask questions and offer the best feedback I can. I understand that collaboration and communication are important to the writing process.

Sample Peer Review

Michigan's Smoking Ban – An Argumentative Research Essay

WRT 160 Student

Cheers ring out throughout the bar; there are whistles and screams in every direction. It is a weekend playoff game for the Detroit Red Wings, and they have just advanced to the next round in their quest for the Stanley Cup. However, it turns out all this excitement in the bar is coming from the television sets all around the establishment. The bar is practically empty with the exception of the lonely bartender who is wondering how long his current job will last. The scenario just provided is completely fictional, fictional yet practical. It is no secret that the state of Michigan has had its fair share of economic problems even before the national recession. Now the burden of opening or God forbid maintaining a small business or establishment is beyond the American dream and is now just a dream. Small time investors and entrepreneurs originally felt safe putting up institutions for customers to come drink, smoke, eat, and be happy. These types of institutions are ideally a safe "bet", meaning the investment put forward practically guarantees return if the food is great and the environment's surroundings are cordial and welcoming. Unfortunately, not only are these specific business owners battling a dreadful economy, but now they also currently have to fight a law passed by the state government of Michigan banning tobacco use in establishments such as bars and restaurants. As mentioned by Jordan Birnholtz (2010), the only businesses exempt from this generally recent law are casinos and specialty smoke shops (para. 1). This is debatable from several different angles. For example, there are those who believe that it is unfair to subject innocent people to ghastly carcinogens in the

| Comment [LR1]: | Your intro is great! It grabs the attention of the reader and gives an anecdotal scenario showing how businesses are affected by the smoking ban. |

| Comment [LR2]: | Be careful not to use leading or biased language. |

| Comment [LR3]: | Is this really true? Can you back this up with research? |

| Comment [LR4]: | Word choice |

| Comment [LR5]: | Word choice |

air they cannot avoid. Another angle taken is that it is also the right however for an owner of an establishment to decide whether or not they wish to allow

Comment [LR6]: This sentence is a little awkward; reword for clarity

patrons to smoke. It is their property, and they believe they have the right to conduct their business any way they wish. From the government's angle, one must feel sympathetic because their only goal is to improve the health of all who

Comment [LR7]: Who?
Comment [LR8]: Only goal?

wish to enjoy themselves in public places and eateries (Birnholtz, 2010, para. 1). This essay will be used as an explorative tool for analyzing and understanding both sides of this controversial issue. First, exploration of the issue in an overview is key to grasping the problem at hand. Next, the stance on the matter will be established to explain and endorse the solution given by the writer for the smoking ban. Therefore, the state of Michigan has absolutely no right to push

Comment [LR9]: Great overview, but can you reword so that this sections reads less like an abstract of your essay?
Comment [LR10]: Reword; extreme language

their way into another's business and conduct it as if it were their own, and also this ban hurts the already crippled economy. However, it would not be fair or credible to simply argue without presenting and explaining the reasoning and facts behind other possible viewpoints and solutions. Then, a rebuttal in the

Comment [LR11]: Combine this with the previous section outlining your essay?

form of a counterargument to the stance will be provided to prove why the stance being taken by opposing views may also be the correct one. Lastly, a possible solution the problem will be provided to compromise or even prove the stance taken by the writer.

Comment [LR12]: This is a great overview of your issue and argument, but this intro seems to be missing a clearly identifiable thesis. Maybe you can rework the overview section and make more concise? You seem to write that both sides will be explored, but the assignment is to create a stance on the issue.

[16]

BEYOND THE COLLEGE ESSAY:
Writing Activities and How They Affect Our Place in Communities

Laura Gabrion and Christina Hall

The goal of a composition class is not simply to teach you how to write successfully in your classes here at Oakland University, but beyond your education and into your post-academic lives. An effective composition course ingrains itself in the way you think and learn, letting you use writing as a tool for discovery and communication. On the surface, college writing experiences are often the same in regards to the process and the final product. You are introduced to a specific discipline, do varying amounts and types of research, and, after peer review and revisions, you are expected to deliver a properly documented, often thesis-driven paper that synthesizes inquiry with findings. The practical value of this type of writing has been demonstrated repeatedly, and writing a research paper forces you to develop and hone a plethora of skills. However, the benefits of a writing course go beyond simply learning good writing habits through skills and processes.

College requires us to fully immerse ourselves in a new environment focused upon intellectual stimulation. In this chapter, we discuss three alternatives to traditional writing in the classroom: campus-based writing, reflective writing, and community-based writing. Campus-based writing includes activities hosted by the Department of Writing and Rhetoric that help you develop and showcase your writing. Reflective writing in first-year writing classes primarily involves writing about your experiences and writing about writing; reflective writing allows you to take an introspective look at the way your writing has developed as well as how your academic and personal life can influence your growth as a reader, critical thinker, and writer. Finally, community outreach and exploratory writing allows you to examine and write about contemporary social issues. Ultimately, when participating in and writing about service and outreach activities, you become informed contributors to the world outside of the university. The various writing activities described throughout this chapter serve to broaden your exposure to these different styles of and purposes for writing. Learning to compose for and in these different situations will also help to strengthen your understanding of rhetorical context and audience. In short, expanding your writing skills will facilitate your ability to communicate original and researched ideas for any audience with any purpose, and becoming a more flexible writer will prepare you for the writing that you will do outside of college.

Campus-Based Writing

"Writing is an exploration. You start from nothing and learn as you go."

– E.L. Doctorow (as quoted in Weber, 1985)

Campus-based writing allows you to develop comfort in the writing process. The Department of Writing and Rhetoric offers several activities that relate directly to writing, including Writing Marathons and Writing Excellence Awards. You explore invention and first drafts in the Writing Marathons, and revision, remediation, and publication for the Writing Excellence Awards. These activities not only celebrate writing and remind you how enjoyable writing can be, but they also give you the opportunity to appeal to a live audience. Through the on-campus writing events, you can also receive valuable feedback. Finally, the responses of your peers help validate your writing and reinforce the fact that what you say *does* matter.

Every semester, our Writing Marathons allow you to explore the campus, use some of its places for inspiration, and connect with a community of other OU writers. Taking place during the fall and winter semesters, our writing marathons consist of three main steps: Walk, Write, and Share. On the day of the marathon, you will be placed in a small group of other writers and, together, decide on an inspiring place to write. As a group, you decide where you are heading. Once you've settled into a cozy or intriguing place, everyone in your group will write whatever comes to mind. There are no guidelines. You may even want to consider writing in a genre or format you've never before written. After your group has written for a short amount of time, you will share what you have written with the group in a comment-free sharing session. Throughout the marathon, your group will wander campus and continue the writing and sharing process. At the end of the marathon, you will have several new drafts of potential stories, memoirs, essays, or poems. Write, read, write, read. Marathons can be an excellent way to cut through your internal censor and give yourself the freedom "to write whatever's on your mind" (Goldberg, 1990, p. 161).

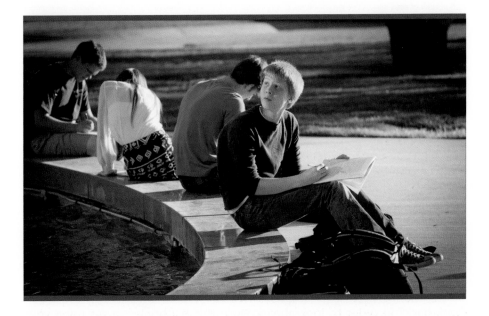

Each year, you have an opportunity to compete for a Writing Excellence Award. Recipients are voted upon by a panel of professors from a variety of disciplines. Writing in six distinct categories can be submitted, ranging from traditional research projects to innovative multi-modal compositions. Awards are granted to the top essays and projects. Monetary awards as well as an honorary luncheon are well-deserved extras. This program celebrates the vast range of writing that you will do at OU, and it encourages you to become an active member of a discourse community within your chosen field of study.

As you participate in actual conversations, you are reminded of the gratification and joy you can feel as a writer and communicator. College life is initially a brand new experience, and clearly, OU provides a variety of opportunities to explore the campus culture. Through these, you take an operative role in becoming a part of the campus community and using the University's many resources. Such self-motivation and adaptability will become even more important in the post-college sphere.

Reflective Writing

> *"Writing is a form of personal freedom. It frees us from the mass identity we see in the making all around us."*
>
> – Don DeLillo (as quoted in Franzen, 1996)

Although you don't always consciously acknowledge it, you reflect on a daily basis, and through your reflections, you grow as an individual. Perhaps you find yourself ruminating over a decision you've recently made or recalling an incident that has deeply affected you. If so, you have begun to explore the value of reflection. Reflective writing allows you to think about what you have learned, assess it, and apply it to other disciplines and topics, and its greatest value is in its ability to guide your thought process.

How do you write a reflection? Most definitely, reflection requires you to "look back" in order to look ahead. Since this textbook focuses upon your growth as a writer, you could first examine past writing assignments. Then, you would respond and reflect by asking yourself questions geared toward helping you to better understand the strategies you've employed and whether or not they've been effective.

Such questions may include:

- Describe your writing process for this assignment, including prewriting, drafting, revising, editing, and collaboration.

- Describe your research process for this assignment, such as locating, evaluating, and integrating sources.

- What are the strengths of your writing in this assignment?

- What parts of your writing in this assignment did you struggle with?

- What did you learn from this writing assignment?

By answering these questions, you will be forced to recall what has worked and what has not, thereby pinpointing effective strategies for future assignments. In critically thinking about and recognizing strengths and weaknesses, you can play on your own strengths in future compositions and know where to work to improve your weaknesses.

Becoming aware of your writing and learning processes and subsequent outcomes consists of three steps: 1) recognizing where you are in regards to strengths and weaknesses, 2) determining how you came to this point, and 3) contemplating where you are going next. For instance, if you apply reflective writing to an understanding of the writing process, you can discover how steps in your writing process affect the outcome of the paper, and then make decisions based on these discoveries to alter or repeat steps.

So far, reflection has been applied specifically to the writing process. However, you know that reflection can also be applied to experiences. In looking at your relationship with others, your situations at home, and your interactions with peers and mentors, you can gain perspective on the types of things that are most important to you. In writing, this moment of discovery is perhaps most critical. You want to write about things that matter to you, and you want your voice to be heard. Through reflection, you will be able to move from broad subject to specific thesis and consider topic, purpose, audience, and approach. You will connect with your assignments because you will value your voice in the conversation that surrounds your topic and your stance. Reflection gives you the reins in your own education; active learners retain and learn more effectively than passive learners.

One of the greatest advantages to reflective writing is its ability to help you transfer knowledge learned from one discipline to the next. In fact, "[scholars] and teachers within the field of composition have long heralded the merits of reflective writing [. . . because] reflecting on their own writing and revision processes is thought to empower students as learners" (Jung, 2011, p. 628). Metacognition, or thinking about thinking, is "the ability to reflect on one's own thinking as well as on the individual and cultural processes and systems used to structure knowledge" (CWPA, NCTE & NWP, 2011, p. 5). Also referred to as "learning about learning," metacognition is "waking up" to the way you think, learn, and write, and reflective writing as a tool helps you discover things about yourself as a thinker, learner, and writer. You can recognize and locate your own personal way of thinking and learning within the larger context of the educational and societal systems you live and work in. According to the *Framework for Success in Postsecondary Writing*, metacognition is one of the eight crucial "habits of mind" that ensure growth and active learning in students (CWPA, NCTE & NWP, 2011, p. 6). Thus, it is through these reflective processes that you take control of your learning and develop a metacognitive set of strategies that will benefit you as you move throughout college and formal education, and beyond into the workplaces and the communities you will inhabit.

Writing Connected to Community Outreach and Exploration

> *"Serving and being served are reciprocal [in] that one cannot really be one without the other"*
>
> – Robert Greenleaf (2002)

Have you ever walked into South Foundation when the front hallway is abuzz with a fund-raising bake sale, or encountered tables set up in the OC enlisting your help with a particular community issue? These students are taking an important first step toward engaging the communities in and beyond OU. You don't have to wait until you leave college to recognize your role as a citizen of an interdependent world. Community-based writing involves working in current social and cultural situations outside of the classroom, and allows you to write about your experiences both academically and reflectively.

Ethnographic studies and service learning take you outside the controlled classroom environment and let you work in the unpredictable, real world. This gives purpose to your writing, and it incorporates research and synthesis, as well as your individual and collective responses to communities or situations and what you'd like to do with those responses. For instance, you can begin by researching a particular community. Perhaps you decide to investigate what causes the high rate of homelessness in Detroit by looking into the history of Detroit, issues of unemployment, drug use, etc. This would be your causal research. You could then look at the effects of homelessness, which could lead you to work at a homeless shelter in the community. This acts as primary research. You go into the experience with certain perceptions based on your preliminary research of the community. Through your new experiences and possible interactions with people from varying perspectives, you can critically reflect on and adjust your conclusions. You could then write a letter, proposal of change or call to action, thus moving your ethnographic study and service learning experiences from purely observational and interactive to proactive.

The educational benefits of service and place-based writing can be seen most efficiently through critical reflection. If you think back to the role reflective writing plays in examining your writing processes, you can apply that concept to your service learning processes as well. It is important to think of reflective writing here as an "intentional and analytic examination" (House, 2012). You can consider the DEAL method of critical reflection: Describe, Examine, Articulate Learning (Ash, Clayton & Moses, 2007). After describing the activity or research, you then examine three areas of enhancement: personal growth, civic engagement, and academic development. Finally, you can articulate your learning, going beyond what you learned, and discuss what you will do with your new knowledge.

The work you do, including writing or learning, does not exist in a vacuum or apart from the communities and cultures you interact within on a daily basis. If you are discussing economic policies or environmental debates, then opinions, perceptions, and outcomes are dependent on the culture they stem from. For example, a discussion of the harmful effects of mining on the environment will be received differently in urban Detroit than it would in a rural mining community in the Upper Peninsula. If you are to write and communicate effectively, you need to have an understanding of the way the culture of communities affects and informs perceptions and audiences. Your awareness of the needs of others, and the reciprocity involved in accepting your ability to affect your social and physical environment are life skills that encourage positive advances and the flexibility crucial to success. Incorporating these activities into writing topics and projects proves that you've connected, assessed, and reported your involvement as well as the effects of it, aptly allowing you to "grow as [a writer and citizen] while working in or with the community" (Amare & Grettano, 2007, p. 57).

Concluding Remarks

It is easy to see the interconnectedness between all three sections of this chapter and how they are both progressive and cyclical. Campus-based writing helps you recognize and build upon your strengths, explore what the campus has to offer, and realize the value in your unique voice. Reflective writing permits you to recognize your place as a writer by contemplating your processes and reflecting on specific assignments. Finally, when you move beyond the campus community and into larger cultures, you acknowledge the interdependency and reciprocity of working in and understanding the world. The more you utilize writing as a tool both inside and outside writing courses and mandatory essays, the more comfortable you become with yourself as a writer, and your writing will help you develop a sense of your role within communities and what they can offer you. Writing is a prime tool within all these instances to both discover and communicate your ideas, allowing you to turn potentially stagnant moments into areas of growth and advancement.

Writing Activities

1. Create a literacy timeline that details significant reading and writing experiences throughout your life. Then expand on one event, what aspects of your life and education influenced it, and how it then in turn affected literacy development.

2. Write a narrative about an event, incident or situation that has happened to you while you've been on campus, and post it on Mapskip.com. Add pictures or videos, too.

3. Service activities provide an excellent opportunity for group work that can be showcased on a class website. Groups can draw connections between any of the following: service-oriented organizations in Oakland County; the activities within the class; the role of the University.

References

Amare, N., & Grettano, T. (2007). Writing outreach as community engagement. *WPA: Writing Program Administration, 30*(3), 57-74. Retrieved from http://wpacouncil.org/archives/30n3/30n3amare-grettano.pdf

Ash, S.L., Clayton, P.H., & Moses, M.G. (2007). *Teaching and learning through critical reflection: An instructor's guide.* Sterling, VA: Stylus Publishing.

CWPA, NCTE, & NWP. (2011). *Framework for success in post-secondary writing*. Retrieved from http://wpacouncil.org/files/framework-for-success-postsecondary-writing.pdf

Franzen, J. (1996, April). Perchance to dream. *Harper's*, 35-54.

Glenn, C. (Ed.). (2011). *The Harbrace guide to writing* (concise 2nd ed.). Belmont, CA: Wadsworth.

Goldberg, N. (2005). *Writing down the bones.* Boston & London: Shambhala.

Greenleaf, R. K. (2002). *Servant leadership: A journey into the nature of legitimate power and greatness* (25th anniversary ed.). New York, NY: Paulist Press.

House, V. (2012, March). Reflective service-learning courses: Gateways to critical thinking. In J. Zimmerman (Chair), *Improving service learning in composition*. Session conducted at the Conference on College Composition and Communication. St. Louis, MO.

Jung, J. (2011). Reflective writing's synechdochic imperative: Process descriptions redescribed. *College English*, *73*(6), 628-647.

Weber, B. (1985, October 20). The myth maker. *New York Times*. Retrieved from http://www.nytimes.com/1985/10/20/books/doctorow-interview1985.html

Part 3:

Writing Excellence Award Winning Essays

[17]

A VALEDICTION FORBIDDING UNANALYZED RHETORICAL AGENDAS

Category 1: Rhetorical Analysis
First Place 2016: Caitlin Keech

The conversation about what media should cover and what should be hidden from the public has been ongoing for the last couple of centuries. There are many who argue that the public should be protected, for its own good, on sensitive topics. There are many others who argue that everybody has a right to the uncensored truth. This is a particular issue with photojournalism. Even media outlets themselves like to speculate about what should be shown. *The New York Times* and *The Week* have published articles explaining why sensitive photos should be released to the public. These articles were published in light of the issue of a circulating photo that shows a Syrian refugee child that died and washed ashore. These two media giants will try to convince their readers that these shocking photos had good reason to be released. Both articles attempt to make the argument in different ways. But it is important that readers analyze the rhetoric of sources covering sensitive topics so they do not get caught up in and swept away by others' views instead of formulating their own.

Media is almost impossible to avoid; we are constantly in contact with some kind of media. Every media outlet readers come in contact with is trying to carry out a rhetorical agenda. Even photojournalists use rhetoric to fulfill an agenda--whether it is to create awareness for a cause or raise money for a company or newspaper. Average readers are pulled in different directions by the rhetoric they come in contact with. Each source is trying to convince its viewer of something. These sources of rhetoric are hoping that their viewer will simply believe in them. The same goes for the rhetoric put forth by *The Week* and *The New York Times*. These specific publications use rhetoric to tell the public what it should think. Some who have not properly learned to analyze rhetoric will let these articles influence their own point of view. But this is easy to avoid; all a reader must do to keep her own views is to more closely inspect the rhetorical tactics. The public itself knows what it can and cannot handle in terms of sensitive photos. It is up to the readers to decode how these articles are trying to convince the public one way or another. Therefore, in order for the public to realize what it truly needs to see from photojournalists documenting tragedy, they must analyze the rhetoric put before them by articles speculating about the topic.

The article published by *The Week,* entitled "Aylan Kurdi, and the Ethics of an Image that Shocked the World" tries to convince its readers that the image of the dead Syrian refugee boy washed ashore being published and spread around is a good thing by using several rhetorical techniques. But the first thing a reader needs to analyze in any article is the ethos, or the legitimacy of the source of information. In this case, the source would be *The Week* and the writer of the article. *The Week* is a sizable British magazine publisher that covers current events. It is a trustworthy source if the reader is looking for information on up-to-date news events. Since the article in question concerns current events, *The Week* can be trusted in their coverage of the sensitivity in the media. The author of the article is Paul Waldman. According to his biography on *The Week's* website, Waldman is a blogger for several news websites and is an author of several books covering media and politics. This makes Waldman an authority on the subject of current events and the ethics of journalism. Examining this information, the ethos of the article is sound.

Further analysis would mean looking at what tactics the article uses to convince its audience. Primarily, the article utilizes pathos. The article tries to appeal to its readers' emotions and capacity for empathy by trying to convince them that the photo of the refugee boy should be shown. The ultimate argument that the article uses is that the photo will inspire action. Waldman confronts the opposing view by calling out that, "the assumption is that images are uniquely persuasive in ways that words aren't, that they not only affect us more viscerally and powerfully right in the moment, but that the impact might turn into some kind of action — opposing a war, or demanding that one's government take a different kind of action when confronting a humanitarian crisis" (Waldman 9). He uses words like "powerful" and "humanitarian crisis" to appeal to his readers' emotions about what can be done to stop this tragedy. The phrase "humanitarian crisis" in particular arouses the feeling that we as humans need to examine this image and realize that we can stop this from happening again and need to help.

Another thing Waldman is doing is trying to use the visual rhetoric involved in the photo to aid in his argument. He recognizes that the picture is more powerful than just a description of the event but argues that this is a good thing because it will bring about change. In itself, the picture in question conveys a message of mournfulness and innocence: this is its visual rhetoric. Waldman is using the photo's visual rhetoric to aid in his own rhetoric. Writers can use the visual rhetoric of the photo for the opposing argument as well, that because the photo shows the loss of innocent life and conveys a message of sadness, the mass sharing of the photo is pervasive. But Waldman writes about the message as a positive. His argument is that the visual rhetoric, and its massive audience, will bring a spotlight on the humanitarian crisis and will inspire the viewers to stop tragedies like these from happening again.

On the other hand, even though the article appeals to pathos, the author also mistakenly quotes the opposition's argument that also uses pathos. As aforementioned, Waldman draws his audience in by convincing them that this is an emotional issue. What he tries to do is convince his readers that their emotions will lead them to the conclusion that the photo of the refugee boy has been rightfully circulated. But Waldman mistakenly quotes convincing pathos evidence from the other side of the argument just as he has drawn the reader in. As soon as the reader is emotionally attached to the argument, Waldman writes that, "people immediately began not just resending the images of his body but repurposing them, making them into cartoons and photoshopping other elements into them" (Waldman 4). If the reader was not emotionally attached, this would have just been another piece of information, but because they are emotionally attached, this becomes a problem. This is a careless use of rhetoric that hurts Waldman's rhetorical argument. An emotionally attached reader does not want to know that the photograph of the little refugee boy has been violated as a result of its distribution. This draws the readers out of the argument and could even convince them of the opposite of what Waldman wants them to feel. It would have been better if Waldman had included evidence from the opposition that used a logos appeal as this would not have drawn his reader out.

The next article to be examined was published by the *New York Times.* "Brutal Images of Syrian Boy Drowned Off Turkey Coast Must be Seen, Activists Say" is also an article that tries to convince its readers that the photograph of the refugee boy should be circulated. Again, this article must be examined for its ethos in order to be deemed legitimate. *The New York Times,* one of the most well-known media outlets in the world, is considered a trusted news source by millions. Since it is a reputable news source with plenty of experience covering current events, its ethos is sound. The author of the article is Robert Mackey. Using a search in *The New York Times* website finds that Mackey has either written or contributed to 2,730 articles. Taking into account that *The New York Times* has been deemed a legitimate media outlet infers that Mackey himself is legitimate, entrusted with covering so many stories. Consequently, *The New York Times* article does have the authority to cover the topic of the circulating picture of the dead refugee boy.

Just as importantly readers must look at what tactics the author uses to convince his readers of his argument. At first glance the article seems to try to appeal primarily to logos, or the reader's logical reasoning. The article quotes numbers such as how twelve people drowned the same day as the little boy. The boy himself was three years old and had a five- year- old brother who also drowned (Mackey 1-3). By giving tragic numbers such as these the author tries to win its audience over; it's seemingly a logical appeal. First, what this does is prove to the reader that the writer has precise information of the event (further establishing the article's ethos). Including these numbers also appeals to the reader by showing them that the little boy in the picture is not the only tragedy that has taken place at this level and the photo needs to be shown so people can be informed when these tragedies do happen so as to prevent them in the future.

Another way that the article seems to appeal to logos is by quoting experts and other news companies on their attitudes. The article lists some prestigious people and media outlets that have issued statements that they are in favor of keeping the photo in circulation. These include the president of the international rescue committee, *Washington Post* correspondents, *The Globe and Mail*, and *The Los Angeles Times* (Mackey). The author is hoping that the reader will logically infer that since these reputable sources take a particular position, so should the reader. By doing so the author is utilizing the "bandwagon" approach: all these people are doing it so you should as well. It's a logical fallacy, a meretricious argument that anybody upon further inspection can unravel. By utilizing these logos tactics the article entices readers into the position that the photo should be circulated.

On closer examination, readers can find that the article primarily uses pathos. The author tries to come off as if he is presenting unbiased facts about the situation that just happened to overwhelmingly conclude in favor of the photo's release being a good event. It is difficult to present a convincing appeal to logos if the speaker is biased. So to remedy that the author tries to appear unbiased, never outrightly stating his position. Yet the article is very biased towards being in favor of the photo's being in circulation. The article never even presents information that is put forth by the opposing argument. The article also only quotes reputable positions that support a specific point of view. In fact, the only argument put forth in the article that supports another side is a Twitter rant of a teenage girl (Mackey 7). Even though Mackey only put information in the article that supports his argument, he still hopes that the reader will read the article thinking that the source is unbiased. Mackey does this because he knows that appearing unbiased will help him and the article, thus helping his logos and ethos. In fact by using this biased information he is more likely grabbing the reader's emotional attention, or pathos. This is another rhetorical tactic that anybody who analyzes the article more closely can pull apart.

In the end, both articles use a pathos appeal. Waldman and Mackey both put up convincing arguments about why the photo of the three-year-old refugee boy drowned and washed ashore should be circulated. Ultimately, both of their arguments are that the photo will inspire change and further injustice. But it is critical that the audience remain aware of how these articles and all other information presented tries to convince them of the authors' beliefs. Rhetoric is being used to convince the viewer that the photo should be circulated and seen by the public. But in reality readers knows what is best for them, and if they let articles like these take away their outlooks, the public loses its power. The power to keep one's own judgment is easily taken away if the reader does not pay attention to rhetorical tactics and agendas. By analyzing the different strategies that rhetoric uses such as ethos, logos, pathos, etc. people can form their own solid conclusions. Readers can decide if an argument is sound using these analysis methods. If an audience fails to properly analyze the rhetoric put before them then their very thoughts are vulnerable to corruptions. Then when thoughts are vulnerable to corruptions, readers falls prey to others' rhetorical agendas. In conclusion, it is imperative that readers analyze any rhetoric put before them in order to retain their own true thoughts.

Works Cited

Mackey, Robert. "Brutal Images or Syrian Boy Drowned Off Turkey Must be Seen, Activists Say" *The New York Times.* 2 September 2015.

Waldman, Paul. "Aylan Kurdi, and the ethics of an image that shocked the world" *The Week.* 4 September 2015.

[18]

PRISON REHABILITATION AND ITS EFFECTS

Category 3: Research Essay
First Place 2015: Elizabeth A. Kellogg

Abstract

In this paper, the issue of increasing prison rehabilitation programs, and the effects they have on both inmates and society are discussed. Since the Progressive movement began in the early 20th century, various attempts at rehabilitating inmates and curbing criminal behavior have been trialed. In recent decades, however, the focus of prisons became not to rehabilitate prisoners, but instead punish them. Recent studies show that this policy has proven to be disastrous, increasing the corrections budget and overpopulating prisons across the nation. This paper explores the recent trends in rehabilitation, provides an insight into how these trends benefit inmates, and how this in turn benefits the American citizen.

Keywords: prison, prison rehabilitation, recidivism

Prison Rehabilitation and Its Effects

America currently houses over 2.4 million inmates, meaning that roughly one in every 100 adults is incarcerated (Petersilia, 2011). With over 19 states operating above their highest capacity (Guerino, Harrison, & Sable, 2012), the prison system is growing at a rate unchallenged by previous years. Major players in the population growth include reoffenders ("The high cost", 2012). These individuals make up the recidivism (reentry into prison) rate. Decreasing the recidivism rate would decrease the prison budget and reduce taxpayer cost. By implementing rehabilitation programs, prisons will reduce the recidivism rate, more adequately treat and understand inmates' mental states and criminal behaviors, and benefit inmates' lives by reeducating them, teaching them job skills, and improving their outlook on life. All U.S. prisons should institute rehabilitation programs to improve the overall health of inmates and better prepare them for reentry into society. Furthermore, instituting rehabilitation programs will allow prisons to more cost-effectively manage their healthcare budgets.

The purpose of sending individuals to prison is to encourage them to reflect on their actions and prevent them from committing crimes in the future. While incarcerated, most mid to low-security inmates have a lot of free time. There are few social opportunities available, and most days are spent doing basic exercises, watching television, if allowed, or playing card games. Rehabilitation programs are beneficial to inmates by giving them constructive ways to spend their time. Successful rehabilitation and social change relies on a change in attitudes, and a change in the inmate's mind (Wilmot, 1976). By encouraging prisoners to have a positive outlook on life, they have an increased sense of self-worth. Reports indicate that "little to no positive effect on inmates," has resulted from the current incarceration system (YvonneG, 2001). While they are being punished, prisoners should be able to have the means to better themselves. Happier prisoners mean that there are fewer disruptions in the prison, lower prison violence, and a positive prison management system. By providing ways to constructively occupy their time, rehabilitation benefits both wardens and inmates (Craig, 2004). A successful prison is one that is not a "total institution," but rather a cooperative institution, in which prisoners are kept occupied, and this in turn contributes to their skills and serves as inmate management during their incarceration (Craig, 2004). In summary, improving an inmate's mental state improves the prison itself, reduces violence, and creates better human beings. From a humanitarian standpoint, rehabilitation is the only way to create positive people post-release.

Drug offenders represent the largest category of offenders in the prison system (Johnson, 2012). Many offenders committed their crime while under the influence of drugs or alcohol, and in 2004, 45% of prisoners met the criteria for drug abuse or dependence (National Reentry Resource Center, n.d.). The addiction does not necessarily stop in prison, where illegal substances can be smuggled in and further escalate the inmate's disease, in addition to creating a hostile and possibly violent environment. Drug and substance abuse programs have been around for decades, but are largely ineffective. A study showed that more than 51,000 inmates were on waiting lists for basic drug education programs (Johnson, 2012). Drugs and drug dependence not only affect the inmate before and during incarceration, but also after release. Offenders who participated in drug or alcohol treatment, community service, and employment programs had recidivism rates 10-20% below those of non-participating offenders (Petersilia, 2011). These results make it obvious that receiving treatment while incarcerated greatly influences whether or not an inmate will return to prison. In 2003, the Bureau of Justice did a study in which it was found that 25% of prisoners being released were determined to be alcohol dependent (Hughes & Wilson, 2003). A staggering statistic, it alludes to the unfortunate cycle of criminal activity and reincarceration that grips hundreds of thousands of people. Addiction interferes with educational and employment opportunities, both which are the core determiners of a successful sojourn into society. If drug and substance abuse were adequately treated in prison, it would lower the chance of released inmates reoffending and increase the probability of prosperity in the outside world.

In addition to providing emotional and mental stimulation while in prison, rehabilitation programs also benefit individuals released from prison. The job training they received will help them acquire a job, something they need to get in order to be successful. The emotional counseling they received will help them sustain positive relationships and encourage social growth. The drug treatment will prevent them from reverting back to their criminal behavior. Many prisons provide reentry programs, which are designed to curb criminal activity and help inmates easily transition into society. Services offered include assistance in job placement, facilitating access to drug-free housing, and providing support systems (Caporizzo, 2011).

In 2001, the Achieving Baby Care Success (ABCS) Program was opened by the Ohio Department of Corrections ("Evaluation of the achieving", 2006). In most cases, children born in prison would be given up to a relative or foster agency. The ABCS Program allows incarcerated mothers to keep their children while living in prison. The goal of the program is to preserve the bond the child has with its mother, which is considered crucial in the first months of development (Stone, 2009). The ABCS Program has been adopted by prisons in Ohio, Nebraska, New York, and Washington state (Ghose, 2002). Babies and their mothers live in a special unit of the prison, where the babies sleep and play and mothers receive a "minimum of 50 hours of parenting education" ("Evaluation of the achieving", 2006) in classes on CPR and how to properly use a car seat. To be accepted into the program, an inmate must have a sentence of less than 18 months, meet established medical and mental health criteria, have no felony convictions, and never have been convicted of a violent crime ("Evaluation of the achieving", 2006). An admissions board reviews the offender's criminal and social history background ("Evaluation of the achieving", 2006). The director of the Ohio Department of Rehabilitation and Correction, Reginald Wilkinson, says, "Prison nurseries benefit the mother, the child, and society as a whole," (Ghose, 2002). The program hopes to keep "the next generation out of prison" (Stone, 2009). Five of the 50 women who participated in the Washington nursery program returned to prison, but none of the participants in the Ohio program did (Ghose, 2002). The recidivism rates of graduates are not stellar, but with refinement and setting more clear goals, the program could improve this rate.

Puppies Behind Bars (PBB) is a nonprofit organization that allows inmates to raise and train service dogs. To be chosen for the program, an inmate goes through a screening process. He must have a clean disciplinary record for at least a year, not committed a violent crime, and pass an interview (Cheakalos, 2004). After being confirmed to the program, an inmate is assigned a puppy and becomes a "primary trainer." (Coeyman, 2000). Puppies and their trainers live in an area separate from the main prison space and spend a year and a half together. Dogs stay with their primary trainer for most of the day, going to prison activities and appointments, while attending training classes during the week. The dogs are trained to be police dogs, bomb-sniffing dogs, and guide dogs for handicapped people (Cheakalos, 2004). In addition to providing the community with a service, the dogs improve inmate morale and help with the rehabilitation process. One participant in the program said, "the canine connection and opportunity to contribute to the outside world has given him a better outlook on life," (Puppy training program, 2014) and the prisoners who participated in the program proved to be more compassionate and responsible (Cheakalos, 2004). By giving them something to care for, inmates are taught responsibility, empathy, and accomplishment. These lessons are indispensable when it comes to leading a positive, adjusted life outside bars. Resident Unit Manager Steve Niemi said prison leader dogs have a "25% higher graduation rate than dogs raised in homes" (Puppy training program, 2014). The $650,000 annual budget comes entirely from donations (Cheakalos, 2004), which makes this a cost-effective program for rehabilitating inmates. PBB is operated out of six prisons in New York, New Jersey, and Connecticut (Cheakalos, 2004), but similar programs have popped up in prisons across the country.

Aside from personal and societal benefits, rehabilitation programs benefit the economy. The problem with the current budget is that it is costing the government 50% more than it did in 2000 (Johnson, 2012). Corrections expenditures fund "community supervision, confinement, and rehabilitation of adults and juveniles convicted of offenses, as well as confinement of persons awaiting trial" (Kyckelhahn, 2014). The prison population is increasing because of new and repeat offenders. The problem with repeat offenders is that the current corrections system clearly did not work for them. The average cost per year to house an inmate was $22,650 ("Why Prison Education? n.d.). The unnecessary years a reincarcerated person is serving in prison are responsible for the increased budget. Inmates are having a problem adjusting to society because of ill-equipped preparation in prison. If more programs became available, inmates would not return to prison, and the budget would be lowered. Rehabilitation programs are economic common sense. By reducing criminal behavior, released inmates are less likely to revert to their prior activities, and less likely to go back to prison. This lowers the recidivism rate, which in turn lowers the prison budget. With less inmates in prison, less funding goes towards feeding and housing them. Less incarcerations also means less legal and court fees, which are often left to the government to pay. America spends over $52 billion dollars on the prison system every year ("The High Cost", 2012), the highest in the world (Petersilia, 2011). The prison system costs quite a hefty sum, and the budget will only become larger following the rapid growth of incarceration rates. The only way to curb the budget is by reducing the recipients of the resources, and rehabilitation has proven to work in reducing the number of reoffenders.

One of the more recent, and most successful, programs currently in place is the Honor Program. Conceived by prisoners and non-custody staff at the California State Prison, Los Angeles County, the program is based on encouraging personal responsibility and making positive behavior an incentive (Hartman, 2007). Almost like a club, it is made up of a racially diverse group of men who want to create a positive, healthy environment. Admission to the program is inclusive, but participants have to abstain from violence, inclusion in gangs, and drugs. Together, the inmates work on community projects and develop techniques to manage their emotional, psychological, social, and vocational health (Hartman, 2007). The program has had an astounding impact on the inmates, as well as the prison. In its first year of operation, it saved the California Department of Corrections and Rehabilitation over $200,000 in costs related to the management of violent and disruptive behavior, as well as decreasing the amount of violent incidents by 85% (Hartman, 2007). By encouraging cohesiveness, the Honor Program has resulted in drastic behavioral change and a more uplifting prison environment. These changes will allow the inmates to smoothly integrate into society with the tools to get and keep a job, exhibit responsible values, and become influential citizens.

Besides inmate care, the prison budget also makes allotments for the "operation and employment of prisons, probation and parole offices, pardon proceedings, correctional administration, and intergovernmental transfer" (Kyckelhahn, 2014). While rehabilitation programs do reduce the prison population, declining numbers of people represent a decrease in the amount of jobs available in the corrections field. If more rehabilitation programs become available, jobs will be eliminated, which does pose a problem. However, prisons exist to punish and rehabilitate criminals, not be involved in the job sector. Looking at the overall benefits to inmates, society, and the economy, rehabilitation is worth it.

To succeed and benefit society, inmates need proper job training. Without employment, released inmates have virtually no choice but to revert back to criminal behavior and become rearrested. High recidivism rates are closely related to the low employment rates among those released from prison (Holzer, Raphael, & Stoll, 2003), and "less than half of released prisoners had secured a job upon their release" (National Reentry Resource Center, n.d.). Ex-offenders face numerous employment barriers, including limited work experience, inability to trust and cooperate with others in the workplace, and the unwillingness of many employers to hire them. Employers view ex-convicts as unreliable and untrustworthy, and are fearful of the legal liabilities that could potentially be incurred (Holzer, Stoll, & Raphael, 2002). Inmates are at a further disadvantage to succeeding because incarceration has proven to reduce former inmates' income by 40% (Western & Pettit, 2010). To combat the low employment rate, prison work programs have increased in popularity and significance. To qualify for participation in these programs, wardens select inmates by considering their behavior, time remaining on their sentence, and the nature of the crime committed (Vu, 2005). In Michigan, prisoners can learn in 13 vocational trade programs, including auto body repair, computer operations, and food service/hospitality management (Michigan Department of Corrections). By becoming certified in their area of expertise, inmates are increasing the likelihood they will become employed upon release. In addition to being a precursor to employment outside prison, work programs instill a sense of personal accomplishment and responsibility in inmates. These rehabilitation programs also lower the corrections budget; each year, Alabama's programs save the state $12 million dollars and California's programs save the state $80 million dollars (Vu, 2005).

Perhaps the most important variable in an inmate's success in the world outside prison is his education level. Of all the inmates in the state and federal prison system, almost 41% have not yet completed high school (Harlow, 2003). Education is fundamental to growth, both inner and outer. To inmates, getting an education gives them an opportunity to acquire social skills, basic strategies for solving personal and work-related problems, and gaining confidence (Tarver, 2001). Prison administrators are often eager to institute rehabilitation programs for prisoners because they know that when engaged in positive behaviors, inmates are "much less likely to act out of control," and "retain a sense of dignity and accomplishment" (Frolander-Ulf & Yates, 2001, p. 115). To the prisons, providing an education to inmates lowers the number of disciplinary infractions and creates a safer, more controlled environment. A study showed that inmates enrolled in college classes committed "75% fewer infractions" than inmates who were not enrolled ("Why Prison Education?" n.d.). Beyond the confines of prison, education has its benefits outside. "Every dollar spent on inmate education . . . meant $4 to $5 not spent on reincarceration down the road," (New York Times Editorial Board, 2014). The more education a person has, the higher their chances are of not being reincarcerated, and a study found that "inmates with at least two years of college have a 10% re-arrest rate, compared to a national rate of 60%" (Frolander-Ulf & Yates, 2001, p. 120).

In the United States, at least 95% of prisoners will eventually be released back to their communities (National Reentry Resource Center, n.d.). More than 50%, however, will be reincarcerated within three years (Petersilia, 2011). Rehabilitation programs should be instituted in all U.S. prisons in order to improve the health of inmates and prepare them for reentry into society, as well as being a viable way to manage the corrections budget. Numerous studies have shown that rehabilitation works, and, as the prison population is rapidly increasing, so too is the corrections budget. If made mandatory in all U.S. prisons, the budget will be reduced, saving the country billions of dollars. By providing rehabilitation programs to inmates, the prison system is allowing them to become positive influences and have an increased sense of responsibility and self-worth. These attitudes determine how successful they will be after release, and are essential for a good life after prison. These programs give inmates a chance to recognize their full potential, and a way to influence the future generation. When inmates can become productive members of society after release, the prison system is doing its job.

References

Caporizzo, C. (2011, November 30). Prisoner reentry programs: ensuring a safe and successful return to the community. *Office of National Drug Control Policy*.

Cheakalos, C. (2004, August). New leash on life. *Smithsonian Magazine*.

Coeyman, M. (2000, August 16). New leash on life. *The Christian Science Monitor*.

Craig, S. C. (2004). Rehabilitation versus control: an organizational theory of prison management. *The Prison Journal, 84*(4), 92-114.

"Evaluation of the achieving baby care success nursery program". (2006, September). Ohio Department of Rehabilitation and Correction.

Frolander-Ulf, M., & Yates, M. (2001). Teaching in prison. *Monthly Review, 53*(3), 114-127.

Ghose, D. (2002, September 24). Nursery program aids jailed moms in four states. *Stateline*.

Guerino, P., Harrison, P. M., & Sable, W. J. (2012). *Prisoners in 2010*. United States of America, Bureau of Justice Statistics, U.S. Department of Justice.

Harlow, C. W. (2003). *Education and Correctional Populations* United States of America, Bureau of Justice Statistics, U.S. Department of Justice.

Hartman, K. (2007). Fast facts and information on the honor program. *The Prison Honor Program*. Retrieved from http://www.prisonhonorprogram. org/Fast_Facts.htm

Holzer, H., Raphael, S., & Stoll M. A. (2003). Employment Barriers Facing Ex-Offenders. *The Urban Institute*, 2-19.

Holzer, H., Stoll M. A., & Raphael, S. (2002). Can employers play a more positive role in prisoner reentry? *The Urban Institute*, 2-10.

Hughes, T., & Wilson, D. J. (2003). *Reentry Trends in the United States* (United States of America, Bureau of Justice Statistics, U.S. Department of Justice).

Johnson, K. (2012, December 4). Prisoners face long wait for drug-rehab services. *USA Today*.

Kyckelhahn, T. (2014). *State Corrections Expenditures, FY 1982-2010* (United States of America, Bureau of Justice Statistics, U.S. Department of Justice). "National Reentry Resource Center Facts and Trends". (n.d.). The Council of State Governments Justice Center.

New York Times Editorial Board. (2014, February 18). Gov. Cuomo's bold step on prison education. New York Times.

Petersilia, J. (2011). Beyond the Prison Bubble. *The Wilson Quarterly (1976-)*, *35*(1), 50–55. Retrieved from http://www.jstor.org/stable/41001069.

Puppy training program brightens life behind bars. (2014, February 10). *The Daily Globe*, *95*(34).

Rosenzwelg, P., Hartman, K. E., & Rideau, W. (2001). Deflating the prison bubble. *The Wilson Quarterly, 35*(2), 5-6.

Stone, G. (2009, January 25). 8 months old and behind bars. *ABC News*.

Tarver, M. L. (2001). Rehabilitation strategies for diverse inmate populations: considerations for recreational therapists, counselors, and educators. *Journal of Correctional Education, 52*(4), 167-171.

"The high cost of corrections in America". (2012, June 12). Pew Charitable Trusts.

United States of America, Michigan Department of Corrections, State of Michigan. (2009). *Academic/Vocational Report.*

Vaccarino, F., & Comrie, M. (2010). Pathway to rehabilitation – prisoners' use of a public library. *The Australian Library* Journal. 54(4), 170-179. http://dx.doi.org/10.1080/00049670.2010.10736022

Vu, P. (2005, February 9). Inmates gladly take on odd jobs for low or no pay. *Stateline.*

Western, B. & Pettit, B. (2010). *Collateral costs: incarceration's effect on economic mobility.* "Why prison education" (n.d.) *Prison Studies Project.*

Wilmot, R. (1976). What is rehabilitation? *International Journal of Offender Therapy and Comparative Criminology, 20*(3), 246-254.

Wolski, K. R., & Murphy, K. (1995). Jail won't cure addiction. *The American Journal of Nursing, 95*(8). http://doi.org/10.2307/3471130

Yvonne, G. (2011, October 13). Rehabilitation in the prison system. *Yahoo Voices.*

[19]

GENETIC MODIFICATION OF CROPS:
A Necessity?

Category 3: Research Essay
First Place 2016: Anthony Polito

Abstract

This paper seeks to address the current state of crop cultivation and development focusing mostly on genetic engineering. The genetic modification (GM) of crops provides many benefits and will be a necessity in coming years. This methodology allows for ideal traits to be expressed in crops resulting in higher quality produce and more efficient cultivation, benefiting both large scale and small-scale farmers. Despite the apparent benefits, many nations around the world have adopted anti-GMO laws for a number of reasons, including an overall negative public view of GM technology. Numerous consumer surveys, such as the nationally conducted survey by the Pew Research center confirmed this viewpoint, although there have been some exceptions. A survey that was conducted for this paper came to the opposite conclusion.

Opponents claim genetic modification is unsafe for many reasons – many of which also claim that Organic alternatives are superior. Critics of Organic farming claim the opposite. A study was conducted that found a common chemical associated with GM foods to be dangerous but extensive review of it revealed numerous methodological flaws resulting in its official retraction. Regardless of any controversy, various expanding global needs have to be addressed and GM technologies look increasingly promising as a solution.

Genetic Modification of Crops: A Necessity?

The world population is growing at an alarming rate: as of October 2015 the total population of the world stood at more than 7.3 billion people ("World Population Clock", 2015). With an ever-growing population, we also face an ever-growing need for food and other cultivated resources. As humanity continues to exhaust what resources are immediately available, it must turn to technology to address our needs. At the forefront of these technologies is the utilization of genetic engineering (GE), or the modification of the DNA of an organism such as corn or cotton, to better suit our needs. The benefits of this technology are vast, ranging from increased productivity and efficiency of crop growth to benefits for the environment. However, as with all emerging technologies, there are skeptics; many have voiced concerns over the safety and efficacy of GE techniques versus conventional and organic methods, as well as raising moral concerns in regards to tampering with nature. In addition to food production, genetic engineering has shown promise in advancing other industries, such as textiles and even medical technologies. Despite the resistance, the genetic modification of organisms has been proven to not only be a safe practice, it is the most effective breeding method for a growing number of crops.

The ability to transfer DNA from one organism to another was first discovered in 1946. Subsequent advances eventually spawned an entire field of biotechnology: genetic modification (GM). Since the 1980s several GM crops have become commercially available: from edible produce such as alfalfa, canola, corn, soy, and tomatoes, to other widely used crops including cotton and tobacco. These crops are bred primarily to improve crop yields in a variety of ways, such as by providing innate resistances to diseases that are normally devastating, by providing the ability to secrete natural pesticides to deter destructive insects, and by giving the ability to resist commercially available herbicides, allowing farmers to more easily control weeds (Bawa and Anilakumar, 2013). These traits give GM crops a clear advantage over conventional ones by allowing farmers to be able to yield a greater percentage of crops that is fit for consumption and reducing what is lost to natural causes. The reduction of waste products immediately benefits both the farmer and the consumer. The farmer has to devote fewer resources to produce the same, if not greater, yields as he or she normally would, and the consumer has a greater supply of crops to access. In areas of the world where crop cultivation is challenging and/or is essential to the livelihoods of many, these effects are even more pronounced. The advent of commercially available GM crops has given small/poorer farms the ability to viably produce what they need even when faced with scarce resources (Bawa and Anilakumar, 2013).

Since its introduction, the utilization of GM technology has been the subject of intense debate with pro and anti-GM groups constantly raising new arguments against one another. Many countries around the world are very cautious regarding the introduction of GM crops into their agriculture – with some disallowing the practice outright – whether it be from wariness due to a lack of understanding, a cultural adherence to traditional practices, or general public outcry (Hossein, 2009). The reaction to GM technology has not been limited to government either. Consumer attitudes of GM food has been negatively affected heavily by anti-GM activist groups who spread their propaganda via various media outlets and take advantage of the public's general ignorance of the mechanisms of GM technology (Bawa and Anilakumar, 2013). Regardless of the overall attitude toward GM technology, experts suggest that education campaigns need to be proliferated and regulation programs need to be introduced to help assuage public fears and wariness (Hossein, 2009).

As stated previously, GM techniques lead to increased yields and lower production costs. In regards to food crops, additional benefits can include higher nutritional content and better taste (Hossein, 2009). However, opponents of GM technology have consistently voiced concerns, many of whom claim that the true safety of GM crops have not been proven thoroughly enough and that they are hazardous to the environment due to pollution via the application of the pesticides/herbicides they have been bred to resist, the possible reduction of ecological diversity, and the potential advent of pesticide/herbicide resistant species due to accidental cross-pollination (Bawa and Anilakumar, 2013). In response to growing concerns regarding the environmental safety of GM technologies, many environmentalist groups have begun pushing for the use of organic farming (OF) and abandoning GM crops altogether (Hossein, 2009). Organic farming follows strict guidelines, forbidding the use of synthetic pesticides and fertilizers, the genetic modification of any produce, and, in the instance of animals, the use of any hormones and antibiotics ("Organic FAQ", 2015). Organic advocates claim that OF practices are easier on small/poor farms because they are closer to traditional farming methods, as well as being better for the environment due to the lack of synthetic pesticides and herbicides. Critics of organic practices have, however, pointed to the decreased yield and efficiency of OF as being unsustainable for farmers trying to subsist on what they grow in addition to making a profit. In addition, many of the organic-allowed, natural alternatives to synthetic pesticides and herbicides are even more toxic than the chemicals OF advocates fear (Hossein, 2009).

Numerous studies have shown that there are no ill-effects as the result of the consumption of GM food (Bawa and Anilakumar, 2013). In response to these, a study was conducted by French molecular biologist Dr. Gilles-Eric Seralini that analyzed the effects of GM corn treated with RoundUp – a popular herbicide that is commonly associated with genetically modified crops – that was consumed by rats. The corn used was bred to resist RoundUp, allowing for farmers to safely utilize the herbicide in their fields without killing off their crop. The study found that a significant portion of the rats developed cancerous tumors and died early when fed the corn over a two year period and concluded that the consumption of "RoundUp Ready" GM corn was hazardous (Jany, 2013). This study is frequently cited by GM opponents when their stance regarding genetic modification is questioned.

After extensive review, however, the study was officially retracted shortly after its publication due to a number of methodological flaws and biases that were present throughout the study. These included sample sizes that were too small, the use of a breed of rats that are known to be highly susceptible to developing cancerous tumors without outside influences, and a shift in the fundamental goal of the study from a toxicological analysis of the herbicide to one focused on the carcinogenicity of the treated corn midway through testing. When these factors were taken into account, the correlation between the consumption of the herbicide-treated corn and the development of tumors was diminished to below what is considered normal tumor development rates for the selected breed of rats. In addition to flaws within the study, there was an alleged confliction of interest – the Seralini research team admitted to being supported by several French organizations that are known to be critical of genetic engineering technologies (Jany, 2013).

As with many controversial technological and scientific advancements, such as stem cell research, GM technology faces a significant hurdle: strong negative public opinion. Spurred on by influence from the public, lawmakers and regulatory agencies may be pressured to implement measures that would be detrimental to the further development of genetic engineering. The following is an analysis of two separate surveys that address public attitudes regarding the genetic modification of crops, one of which was conducted by the Pew Research Center, the other specifically for this paper.

Method 1: Data Analysis of Pew Research Survey

Participants

The participants of this study consisted of U.S. adults that had access to a landline or cell phone. There were 2,002 respondents in total. Participants were selected such that African Americans and Hispanics were disproportionately represented to obtain a greater number of responses from each group. Aside from the aforementioned exceptions, the respondents were chosen to represent the population of the U.S. as a whole (Pew Research Center, 2015). (See Appendix A).

Instrumentation

Participants were first verified to be of the desired demographic and then asked a series of questions regarding their stances on select topics (Pew Research Center, 2015). (See Appendix A)

Data Collection

Interviewers contacted potential respondents via phone call. The survey asked for thoughts on a wide variety of political and scientific topics, but for this analysis we are only looking at attitudes regarding the genetic modification of food (Pew Research Center, 2015). (See Appendix B).

Data Analysis

Responses showed that 57% of respondents believe that it is "generally unsafe" to eat genetically modified foods. Women were more likely to be against the consumption of food than men (65% versus 49%). Responses were largely the same across all age groups. Results found that, with the exception of those in possession of a postgraduate degree, all education levels had a majority that believed the consumption of GM food to be unsafe (57% of postgraduate degree holders believed them to be safe for consumption). The study also revealed that only 28% of the respondents "believe that scientists have a clear understanding of the health effects of GM crops." This trend is similar across all demographics with the older respondents being more likely to have this view (72% of the 65+ group) than the younger respondents (61% of the 18-29 group). 69% of all respondents also believe that consuming foods treated with pesticides to be unsafe (Pew Research Center, 2015) (See Appendix B).

Results

By a significant margin, the majority of U.S. adults do not feel that the consumption of genetically modified crops is safe and also believe that the scientific consensus is that they are unfit for consumption. This sentiment is shared across all demographic groups (with the exception of postgraduate degree holders) with only some variability (Pew Research Center, 2015).

Method 2: Opinion Survey

Participants

The participants of this study consisted primarily of college students enrolled in the WRT 160 class at Oakland University in addition to several unidentified individuals polled via social media. Thirty-seven individuals responded to the survey in total. General demographic information of the participants is unknown (the survey did not ask for personal information).

Instrumentation

Participants were asked a series of four questions with an optional comment section at the end. Question one required a simple yes/no response while questions 2-4 asked participants to rank their views of a statement from 1 to 5. The optional comment block allowed for survey takers to leave any additional remarks/comments regarding the topic of the survey (see Appendix C).

Data Collection

A link to the survey was posted via the classroom discussion forums as well as via social media (Facebook). Responses were collected over the course of one week.

Data Analysis

24 respondents (65% of survey takers) responded yes to question one. Using the 1 to 5 scale, questions 2, 3, and 4 averaged a 2.94, 3.54, and a 2.9, respectively. Only 7 participants opted to leave a remark in the comment block (See Appendix D).

Results

The survey revealed that the majority of respondents support the genetic modification of crops for human use (23 respondents), they believe the technology is at least somewhat safe (24 respondents), and that the technology has been fairly researched (19 respondents). The comments left by participants showed they had a neutral and cautious stance. One respondent, for example, said,

Gene splicing to create or eliminate certain traits has been shown to be pretty safe overall. Using various "chemicals" (again, in this case chemicals being another general blanket term) to alter the way a crop is grown could be safe or disastrous if not overlooked by competent scientists or other qualified professionals. It was only through genetic modification we have certain crops anyway. The bananas we eat considering there are species of the banana we used to eat that have gone extinct is such an example. The size and heartiness of our potatoes would never have been anything close to what we take for granted today if not for genetic modification. There are dangerous methods to anything. We should always be making sure we're not causing more destruction when we're trying to help a cause. Genetic modification on the whole is one of them (personal communication, November 8, 2015).

While not as in depth, other respondents shared similar sentiments. These responses echo the results of the survey. Most responses were 2, 3, or 4 on the 1-5 scale.

Limitations

Due to the limited time frame and the limited options for distributing the survey, the desired number of survey takers was not obtained. As a result, the sample size may be too small to truly represent the views of the populace regarding genetic modification. Changes to the survey could have been made that would have provided demographic information of the respondents. Such information would have helped to categorize responses.

Discussion

Contrary to many of the nationally conducted surveys, such as the Pew Research study, the survey conducted for this paper showed a more favorable view of genetic modification than has been reported. However, the number of responses to this survey was very small in comparison (only 36 responses for this survey vs thousands for those conducted nationally). Had the second survey had a number of participants similar to or even greater than the Pew survey, it is possible that the results could have been very different and reached a similar conclusion to that of the Pew survey.

Genetic modification has existed in at least some way throughout the entirety of human civilization. However it is only within recent decades that man has been able to directly manipulate the genetic makeup of an organism. Despite being relatively new in comparison to previous practices, the process is highly precise – many times more than the traditional practice of crossbreeding members of one species (Hugi, 2010). While many currently oppose the technology for a wide variety of reasons (many of which are unfounded), one fact remains clear – humans as a species are going to be facing a crisis in the near future if a method for cultivating food is not secured due to the steadily increasing population. GM crops are currently being argued as the future of agriculture in a world where the demand for food is increasing substantially every year (Hussein, 2009).

References

Bawa, A. S., & Anilakumar, K. R. (2013). Genetically modified foods: Safety, risks and public concerns—a review. *Journal of Food Science and Technology, 50*(6), 1035–1046. http://doi.org/10.1007/s13197-012-0899-1 Current World Population. (2015). Retrieved from http://www.worldometers.info/world-population/

Hossein, A. (2009). Genetically modified and organic crops in developing countries: A review of options for food security. *Biotechnology Advances, 28*(1), 160-168. doi:10.1016/j.biotechadv.2009.11.003

Hugi, M. (2010). There's no need to fear genetically modified food. *Medical Post, 46*(16), 11. Retrieved from http://www.canadianhealthcarenetwork.ca/

Jany, K. (2013). Critical remarks on the long-term feeding study by Séralini et al. (2012): Does the study provide proof of health threats posed by genetically modified foods? *European Food and Feed Law Review, 8*(3), 176-186. Retrieved from http://effl.eu/

Organic.org - Organic FAQ. (2015). Retrieved from http://www.organic.org/home/faq

Pew Research Center. (2015). Americans, Politics, and Science Issues. 127-140, 152-158. Retrieved from http://www.pewinternet.org/files/2015/07/2015-07-01_science-and-politics_FINAL.pdf

Appendix A

Appendix A: About the General Public Survey

The bulk of the analysis in this report stems from a general public survey conducted by telephone with a national sample of adults (18 years of age or older) living in all 50 U.S. states and the District of Columbia. The results are based on 2,002 interviews (801 respondents were interviewed on a landline telephone and 1,201 were interviewed on a cellphone). Interviews were completed in English and Spanish by live, professionally trained interviewing staff at Princeton Data Source under the direction of Princeton Survey Research Associates International from Aug. 15 to Aug. 25, 2014.

Survey Design

A combination of landline and cell random digit dial (RDD) samples was used to reach a representative sample of all adults in the United States who have access to either a landline or cellular telephone. Both samples were disproportionately stratified to increase the incidence of African American and Hispanic respondents. Within each stratum, phone numbers were drawn with equal probabilities. The landline samples were list-assisted and drawn from active blocks containing one or more residential listings, while the cell samples were not list-assisted but were drawn through a systematic sampling from dedicated wireless 100-blocks and shared service 100-blocks with no directory-listed landline numbers. Both the landline and cell RDD samples were disproportionately stratified by county based on estimated incidences of African American and Hispanic respondents.

Interviewing Procedures

All interviews were conducted using a Computer Assisted Telephone Interviewing (CATI) system, which ensures that questions were asked in the proper sequence with appropriate skip patterns. CATI also allows certain questions and certain answer choices to be rotated, eliminating potential biases from the sequencing of questions or answers.

For the landline sample, half of the time, interviewers asked to speak with the youngest adult male currently at home and the other half of the time asked to speak with the youngest adult female currently at home, based on a random rotation. If no respondent of the initially requested gender was available, interviewers asked to speak with the youngest adult of the opposite gender who was currently at home. For the cellphone sample, interviews were conducted with the person who answered the phone; interviewers verified that the person was an adult and could complete the call safely.

Appendix B

Safety of Eating Genetically Modified Foods

% of U.S. adults who say it is generally safe/unsafe to eat genetically modified foods

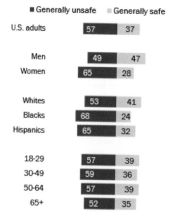

Survey of U.S adults Aug. 15-25, 2014. Q38. "Don't know" responses not shown. Whites and blacks include only non-Hispanics; Hispanics are of any race.

PEW RESEARCH CENTER

Differing Views About Safety of Eating Genetically Modified Foods, by Education and Science Knowledge

% of U.S. adults who say it is generally safe/unsafe to eat genetically modified foods

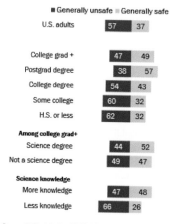

Survey of U.S adults Aug. 15-25, 2014. Q38. "Don't know" responses not shown.

PEW RESEARCH CENTER

Views on Scientific Understanding of GM crops

% of U.S. adults who say scientists have a clear/not clear understanding of the health effects of GM crops

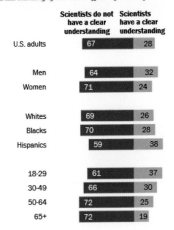

	Scientists do not have a clear understanding	Scientists have a clear understanding
U.S. adults	67	28
Men	64	32
Women	71	24
Whites	69	26
Blacks	70	28
Hispanics	59	38
18-29	61	37
30-49	66	30
50-64	72	25
65+	72	19

Survey of U.S. adults Aug. 15-25, 2014. Q39. "Don't know" responses not shown. Whites and blacks include only non-Hispanics; Hispanics are of any race.

PEW RESEARCH CENTER

Eating Foods Grown With Pesticides

% of U.S. adults saying it is generally safe/unsafe to eat foods grown with pesticides

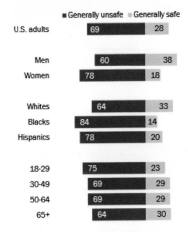

■ Generally unsafe ■ Generally safe

	Generally unsafe	Generally safe
U.S. adults	69	28
Men	60	38
Women	78	18
Whites	64	33
Blacks	84	14
Hispanics	78	20
18-29	75	23
30-49	69	29
50-64	69	29
65+	64	30

Survey of U.S. adults Aug. 15-25, 2014. Q35. "Don't know" responses not shown. Whites and blacks include only non-Hispanics; Hispanics are of any race.

PEW RESEARCH CENTER

Appendix C

Opinion of Genetic Modification

For this survey, consider "genetic modification" to mean purposely modifying the genetic makeup of an organism by adding/subtracting specific genes in a laboratory setting

* 1. Do you support the use of genetic engineering to modify crops (crops being any plant cultivated for human use)?

○ Yes

○ No

* 2. On the following scale, how do you feel regarding the safety of genetic modification?

1: Not safe at all	2	3: Somewhat safe	4	5: Completely safe
○	○	○	○	○

* 3. On the following scale, how thoroughly do you feel genetic engineering technology has been researched (safety, effectiveness, etc)?

1: Little to no research	2	3: Somewhat researched	4	5: Extensively researched
○	○	○	○	○

* 4. On the following scale, how do you feel the government should treat GM technology?

1: No regulation/restrictions	2: Little regulation/restrictions	3: Some regulation/restrictions	4: Heavy regulation/restrictions	5: Completely ban all GM technology
○	○	○	○	○

5. Any additional opinions/remarks are welcome!

[Done]

Department of Writing and Rhetoric

Appendix D

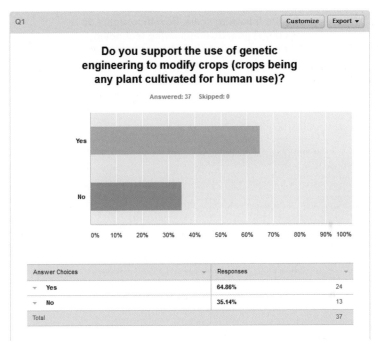

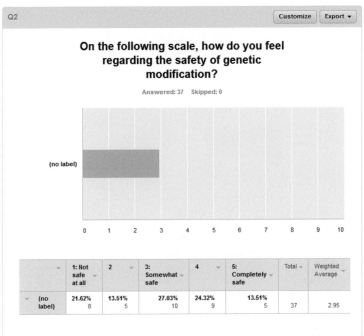

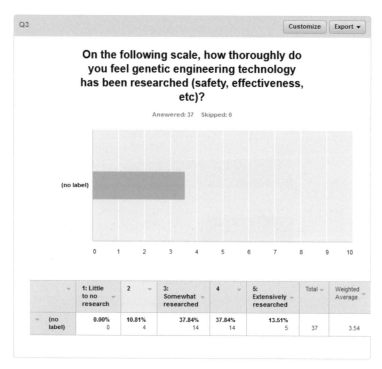

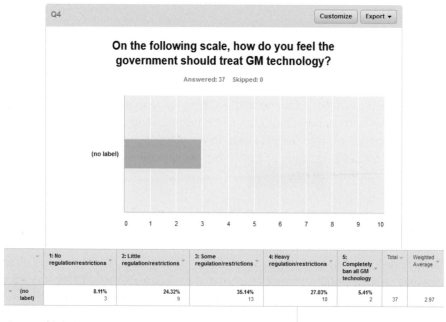

[20]

THE ACTUAL LAST, FINAL REFLECTION:
Composing a Research Paper

Category Eight: Reflective Writing
First Place 2016: Emily Stamper

Throughout the course of Writing 160, my thoughts and feelings towards rhetoric elements and aspects, such as audience, media, synthesizing, and revising, have changed. This is mostly due to the fact that prior to this class the only kind of rhetoric I knew was a rhetorical question; which, despite its name, doesn't really have anything to do with writing and rhetoric. So most of the information I learned was new to me; I knew how to write well, but I had never considered many of the things one should when making a video, especially a persuasive one.

Making a Persuasive Video[1]

Before this class I had never made a video; nothing even remotely close. I am the least artistic person I know, and I had always considered making a video a form of art. So, with my track record in the arts being not so stellar, I had nev-

---

1 This essay has been adapted from a blog post that can be read in its original format at this address: https://emilystamperwrite.wordpress.com/2015/12/09/the-actual-last-final-reflection-making-a-persuasive-video/

er even attempted to make one. I wasn't expecting to have to make a video in a writing class, so I was mostly terrified at the prospect of creating one. My first attempt at making a short video didn't go too well; I hadn't even opened a new project and was extremely frustrated when nothing happened when I tried to insert my media. After twenty minutes of frustrated clicking, I asked my professor what I was doing and realized that I was completely useless at making videos, as shown by my first attempt, which I will link here.

This short clip looks just like a first time video should: no transitions, boring text, generic music, and no cohesive flow. And it most certainly does not convince anyone of the importance of animal shelters. The reason I chose to link it was to show how important composition process, rhetoric, and compositional techniques are when trying to convey a message.

Once I learned how to use iMovie, the whole process was much smoother, which made it easier to focus on the rhetorical elements of the video, such as the rhetorical triangle and logos, pathos, and ethos. What really helped me to understand how to effectively use these rhetorical elements was analyzing other students' works and figuring out what techniques they used. This is an excerpt from reading response eight, where I analyzed a video about gender equality in sports.

"Possibly if she had included more instances where this inequality was evident, it might be easier to take this issue seriously, but, as it were, it seemed at some points she was making some excuses for why female athletes are treated this way, which took away from her argument. I think she had good kairos in her video, as this is a prevalent issue, but she lacked some aspects of pathos that would have made her video a bit more successful in delivering her message. Her logos was decent: showing what a google search turns up is a logical way of showing the differences in the perceptions of male versus female athletes."

Watching other students' work was an important part of the composition process because it gave me an idea of where to go with my own video and allowed me to see what was effective and what was not. Based on my observations, I made these goals.

Compositional Process and Compositional Techniques

The first thing I thought about when I began the process of making my video was the visual elements; what kinds of pictures and videos would be most effective. To determine this, I utilized the CRAP principles we learned in class and felt that contrast and repetition would be most useful in my piece. I found pictures with contrast, before and after photos of abused dogs, and showed them throughout the video to constantly remind my audience that there are animal that need the help that shelters provide. Logos was an important part of my video. I also relied heavily on pathos in the beginning of the video, using plenty pictures of sad, abused animals and a Sarah McLachlan song; the same one used in every animal shelter commercial ever. However, after a conference with my professor, I revised the video and changed out the song. The Sarah McLachlan song was too recognizable and may have caused some-one watching it to tune out, as they had probably heard that song a hundred times on TV and figured this video would be no different. After changing to a less recognizable but equally sad song, I was more confident in the appeal to pathos. Click here and watch about the first thirty seconds, which will show the effect of the new song.

The whole process of making a video taught me a lot about my own compos-ing process, which is something that I had never really thought about before; especially my process for composing a video. Before, I had always just dove right in; not really giving much thought to audience or rhetorical purpose and just simply addressing the prompt. After Writing 160, I have a better under-standing of how to properly prepare for rhetorical works.

Composition Process and Techniques

I had more of an actual process for writing a paper than for making a video prior to this class, but it wasn't very thorough. In high school, to prepare for an essay I just thought of what I wanted to talk about and I might have writ-ten some sort of (really) rough outline and that was it. I didn't think about the rhetorical triangle; I didn't use any drafting or editing techniques. And for high school level essays that was enough. However, I knew that would have to change in college, but before Writing 160 I never really knew how.

One technique that really helped me plan out my essay and organize my thoughts was free writing. While I had never tried that sort of approach before, I found that simply letting the thought flow was helpful. When I was first planning out my paper, I didn't even know what I wanted my thesis to be; I knew it was going to do with animal shelters but I had no idea what aspect to focus on. But when we had to free write for five minutes in class and I started rambling on about animal shelters I noticed a pattern in my writing: I had a lot of facts to support no kill animal shelters but little to no information about kill shelters. This is what I decided to base my thesis on: arguing which type of shelter is more beneficial to animals and society. Before I began writing, I made a goal for myself, which you can view here. I feel that goals are important to have when writing because they give you something to work towards.

As I began writing my rough draft, I thought about what rhetorical appeals would be best suited to my essay. After learning about so many in class and implementing them in my works throughout the semester it wasn't too difficult. I considered my audience; in this case those involved in the kill/no kill shelter debate, and tailored my writing towards them, making sure not to belittle anyone's views while still refuting them. For example this quote from my paper, "The current arguments against each type of shelter are all valid, which makes it difficult to pick one over the other," allows me to insinuate that there are problems with each argument but still give credence to their arguments. I also wanted to incorporate a lot of logos in my paper in order to boost my ethos. So while I relied on more pathos for my video, I found that the appeal to logos was more helpful in my paper. Especially for an audience that is so focused on morals, a dose of logic is good.

Another technique I found to be helpful was learning how to weave quotes, as I was unfamiliar with how to properly introduce quotes. One of my goals for my paper was to introduce all of my quotes through weaving and my professor said that I "use weaving very well with quotations." Which is an example of how my writing has changed over the semester, as I used to just throw my quotes in my paper with little thought, but now I know how to properly introduce them, as well as lead the reader away from them.

In terms of my writing in the future, I feel the skills I learned in this class will be invaluable, but what I think will be most helpful will be my new understanding of the rhetorical triangle. What's the point of writing an essay if it doesn't appeal to your audience?

This class has also shown me when to use words to convey a message and when to use a video. I have found that when attempting to appeal to emotions, a video is a more effective way of communicating. The ability to use sound and images in a video allows the audience to easily visualize and feel what you are talking about. However, when trying to appeal to someone's logical side, I think writing is more convincing. Writing appears more professional and put together, and the way sources are cited in a paper lend themselves better to research.

Part 4:
Academic Style Guides

[21]

MLA DOCUMENTATION GUIDE

MLA Style

For MLA style, you may refer to the *MLA Handbook for Writers of Research Papers* and the MLA website, http://www.mla.org. The Purdue Owl, https://owl.purdue.english.edu, is also an excellent reference.

A paper written in MLA style should be double-spaced, with margins set at one inch on all sides. Choose a standard typeface such as Times Roman in 12 pt. type.

Beginning on the first page, generate a heading on the upper right-hand side of the page that gives the page number.

Do not create a cover page unless your instructor specifies one. Instead, on the upper left-hand side of the first page, give your name, your instructor's name, the course, and the date. These items should all be flush left, double-spaced, and set on separate lines.

Double-space again and center the title. Follow the title with another double-space and indent the first line of text. Indent each paragraph.

Bibliographical Documentation

In MLA style, this is called the Works Cited page. The title, Works Cited, should appear centered on the top margin of the last page of a researched essay. The Works Cited page should be double-spaced with no extra line spacing between entries. The first line of each entry begins at the margin, and all subsequent lines of a particular entry are indented 5 spaces on the left margin. All entries should be in alphabetical order. If your instructor requires that you write an Annotated Bibliography you will format it the same way you format a Works Cited page. The only difference is that you will add an annotation describing the source in a paragraph following the citation. The following entries are typical citations prepared according to MLA style. Examples are offered for print, online, and database versions, when applicable.

Book

Egan, Jennifer. *A Visit from the Goon Squad*. New York: Knopf, 2010. Print.

Book with Two Authors

Friedman, Thomas L., and Michael Mandelbaum. *That Used to Be Us: How America Fell Behind in the World It Invented and How We Can Come Back*. New York: Farrar, Straus and Giroux, 2011. Print.

Two or More Selections from the Same Print Collection or Anthology

Note: To avoid repetition on the list of works cited, cite an anthology or reader as a separate entry. Then cross-reference entries to the anthology as in the example below.

Burns, Gary. "Marilyn Manson and the Apt Pupils of Littleton." Petracca and Sorapure 284–90.

Fox, Roy. "Salespeak." Petracca and Sorapure 56–72.

Petracca, Michael, and Madeleine Sorapure, eds. *Common Culture: Reading and Writing About American Popular Culture*. 5th ed. Upper Saddle River: Pearson, 2007. Print.

> **Note**: Alphabetize each entry among other entries on the Works Cited page. Do not group the entries from the anthology together unless they fall next to one another alphabetically. Also, remember that you will have no parenthetical citation referencing the editors Petracca and Sorapure. You should cite Burns and Fox in the parenthetical citations in your paper.

Book with Multiple Editors

Mennuti, Rosemary B., Arthur Freeman, and Ray W. Christner, eds. *Cognitive-Behavioral Interventions: A Handbook for Practice*. New York: Routledge, 2006. Print.

Online Edition of Book or Novel

James, Henry. *The American*. 1877. *Fiction: The Eserver Collection*. Web. 15 June 2008.

> (This book was published before 1900, so the name and city of the publisher are not needed. For more recent books, give the print information first, then the information about web publication.)

Macfie, Alexander Lyon, ed. *Orientalism: A Reader*. New York: New York UP, 2000. *Google Books*. Web. 26 Sept. 2011.

Scholarly Article in Print Journal

Thompson, Jason. "Magic for a People Trained in Pragmatism: Kenneth Burke, and the Early 9/11 Oratory of George W. Bush." *Rhetoric Review* 30.4 (2011): 350–71. Print.

Scholarly Article Found in Online Database

Angel, Ronald J. "Immigrants and Welfare: The Impact of Welfare Reform on America's Newcomers." *Contemporary Sociology: A Journal of Reviews* 39.5 (2010): 568–69. *Academic Search Complete.* Web. 10 Sept. 2011.

Scholarly Article from Journal Published Online

Gustafsson, Amanda. "Beware the Invisible." *Papers from the Institute of Archeology* 20 (2010): n. pag. Web. 29 Sept. 2011.

> **Note**: MLA specifies including page numbers for scholarly publications, so if the online journal does not provide page numbers, include n. pag. (no page).

Book Review

Schneider, Robert J. Rev. of *Modern Physics and Ancient Faith*, by Stephen M. Barr. *Anglican Theological Review* 86 (2004): 506–07. Print.

Book Review Published Online

Garner, Dwight. "An Unearthed Treasure That Changed Things." Rev. of *The Swerve: How the World Became Modern. New York Times.* New York Times Co., 27 Sept. 2011. Web. 28 Sept. 2011.

An Editorial

Wolfe, Gregory. "The Operation of Grace." Editorial. *Image: A Journal of the Arts and Religion* 70 (Summer 2011): 3–4. Print.

An Editorial Published Online

"U.S. House: Members Are Not as Uncivil as They Seem." Editorial. *Nation Now. Los Angeles Times*, 28 Sept. 2011. Web. 29 Sept. 2011.

Note: This editorial was published in a blog called *Nation Now* that is published by the *Los Angeles Times*.

Magazine Article

Perry, Alex. "Epidemic on the Run." *Time* 26 Sept. 2011: 46–49. Print.

Magazine Article from Online Database

Neuwirth, Robert. "Global Bazaar: Shantytowns, Favelas and Jhopadpattis Turn Out to Be Places of Surprising Innovation." *Scientific American* Sept. 2011: 56–63. *Academic Search Complete*. Web. 29 Sept. 2011.

Online Magazine Article

Leonard, Andrew. "Inside the Shadow Economy: The Growing Underwater Bazaar." *Salon*. Salon Media Group, 29 Sept. 2011. Web. 29 Sept. 2011.

Note: The title of the magazine is followed by the publisher or sponsor of the site, a comma, and the date of publication. MLA uses this format because it does not consider online-only magazines to be periodicals. If no publisher is given, add n.p., and if no date is given, add n.d.

Published Interview

"Samantha Stosur, U.S. Open Champion." Interview by Cassandra Murnieks. *Time*. Time Inc., 23 Sept. 2011. Web. 29 Sept. 2011.

Personal Interview

Doe, Jane. Personal interview. 30 May 2015.

Online Speech

King, Martin Luther, Jr. "I Have a Dream." Speech. March on Washington for
Jobs and Freedom. Lincoln Memorial, Washington, D.C. 28 Aug. 1963.
Americanrhetoric.com. Michael E. Eidenmuller, n.d. Web. 29 Sept. 2011.

> **Note**: The citation includes n.d. (no date) because the date when
> the speech was posted on the site is not given.

Page on a Website

Coe, Jennifer. "How to Refinish a Dresser." *How To*. SheKnows LLC, 3 Aug.
2011. Web. 29 Sept. 2011.

> **Note**: The blog *How To* lists its publisher as SheKnows LLC. If the
> publisher were not given, then you would use n.p. (no publisher).

Image from a Website

Van Gogh, Vincent. *Cypresses*. 1889. Oil on canvas. *The Metropolitan Museum
of Art*, New York. The Metropolitan Museum of Art. Web. 29 Sept. 2011.

Blog Posting

"Respect Your Audience." *Writer's Block*. NIVA Inc., 2009. Web. 15 Sept. 2011.

> **Note**: The blog does not list an author for the posting, so the cita-
> tion begins with the title.

Government Document

El Chamizal Dispute: Compliance with Convention of the Chamizal. 1964. *U.S.
Senate Hearing*. Cleofas Calleros Papers. University of Texas at El Paso
Library Special Collections. 33–9. Print.

Government Document Online

Travis, William Barret. *Letter from the Alamo, 1836.* Texas State Library & Archives Commission. Web. 15 Apr. 2011.

Government Document from Online Database

"United Nations Resolutions on Operation Desert Storm." Aug–Nov 1990. *Essential Documents in American History: 1492–Present.* 1–17. *Academic Search Premier.* Web. 8 May 2011.

A Film on DVD

The Lord of the Rings: The Return of the King. Dir. Peter Jackson. New Line, 2003. DVD.

Television Program

Martin, David. "The Pentagon's Ray Gun." *60 Minutes.* CBS. New York, 2 Mar. 2008. Television.

MLA Parenthetical or (In-Text) Documentation

Parenthetical documentation refers to the process of citing sources within the text. Citing sources within the text is necessary for students to indicate when they are using the words, thoughts, or ideas that are not their own and borrowed from an outside source. Whether students use a direct quote, a paraphrase, or a summary of the information, they must properly provide credit to the original author(s) of that source. Using appropriate sources for support and documenting these sources accurately adds to the credibility and value of a student's essay. The following examples provide a guideline to proper parenthetical documentation.

Direct Quote (four lines or less)

"Scientists estimate that the rangewide population of the San Joaquin kit fox prior to 1930 was 8,000 . . . " (Conover 44).

Direct Quote (more than four lines)

Conover's 2001 study of the San Joaquin kit fox found the following:

> For the most part, in the "real" world, kit foxes escape their pred-
> ators and the high temperatures of their desert environment by
> spending the day underground in a den. In Bakersfield, they follow
> suit. Kit foxes move every couple of weeks to a new den. Moving
> to different dens may be one reason why they have persisted; the
> constantly changing abodes provided new places to hide. (199)
>
> **Note**: For a direct quote that is more than four lines, the passage
> should be indented one inch from the left margin spaces and set as
> a block, as shown here.

Direct Quote When the Author Is Named in the Text

Hildebrand states that "generals of Alexander the Great brought news to Europe of vegetable wool which grew in tufts of trees in India" (144).

Information from Printed Source (but not a direct quote)

It is common to see an Osprey make its nest on an electric power pole (Askew 34).

Electronic Sources

Many electronic sources are not numbered with pages unless they are presented in a PDF file. If paragraphs are numbered, use numbers following the
abbreviation, par. Most often the source will not have page, paragraph, section, or screen numbers.

When numbered paragraphs are cited, add a comma after the author's last
name: (Last, par. 1). Use pars. for more than one paragraph: (Last, pars. 2-3).

When no page numbers, paragraph numbers, or sections are available, use
only the author's last name: (Coe).

[22]

APA DOCUMENTATION GUIDE

APA Style

For APA style, you will want to refer to the *Publication Manual of the American Psychological Association* and the website provided by the American Psychological Association, http://www.apastyle.org, which offers free tutorials for APA style. The Purdue Owl also offers excellent information at https://owl.english.purdue.edu.

APA specifies that your essay should be typed in 12 pt. Times Roman type and double-spaced, with one-inch margins. In addition, APA style specifies the following general rules for formatting a paper or essay:

- Running heads—Create running heads for your page numbers, flush left, beginning on the title page. Also, on the title page, you should have a running head that reads like this:

  Running head: ABBR. TITLE

  with the title actually being your paper title. On succeeding pages, the flush left header should include only the page number and the shortened or abbreviated title, not the words "Running head."

- Title page—In addition to the running heads, your title page will contain the title of the paper (one- or two-line title), followed by your name on the second line, and then the name of your college on the third line, all centered.

- Unless your instructor specifies otherwise, the second page of your paper is a 150- to 200-word abstract that summarizes the major aspects of your paper. The abstract should be double-spaced, in block form, and include the title Abstract (centered at the top of the page).

- Your essay will begin on page 3. This is where you will put the full title of your paper, centered on the first line of the page. Every paragraph after that should be indented and double-spaced.

- At the end of your paper, include your References, which lists your sources according to APA citation style.

Bibliographical Documentation

In APA style, this is called the References. The title, References, should appear centered on the top margin of the last page of a researched essay. The References page should be double-spaced with no extra line spacing between entries. The first line of each entry begins at the margin, and all subsequent lines of a particular entry are indented on the left margin 5 spaces for a References page. All entries should be in alphabetical order. If you are required to write an Annotated Bibliography, it will be formatted like the References page with the addition of an annotation or description of the source in a paragraph following each citation.

> **Note**: APA suggests that when you are citing a source from the web or an online database you should give the DOI (Digital Object Identifier) of the source in the References list. If the DOI is not available, you can give the URL (web address) for the journal's home page. APA does not require that you give the date you access a source on the Internet unless you have reason to believe that the text may change or disappear from the Internet. Also note that if you cite an entire website, simply include the website address in parentheses in the text with no entry in the References page. The following entries are typical citations for APA style. Examples are offered for both print, online, and database versions, when applicable.

Book

Egan, J. (2010). *A visit from the Goon Squad*. New York: Alfred A. Knopf.

Book with Two Authors

Friedman, T. L., & Mandelbaum, M. (2011). *That used to be us: How America fell behind in the world it invented and how we can come back*. New York: Farrar, Straus & Giroux.

Book with Multiple Editors

Mennuti, R. B., Freeman, A., & Christner, R. W. (Eds.). (2006). *Cognitive-behavioral interventions in educational settings: A handbook for practice*. New York: Routledge.

Electronic Books

Macfie, A. L. (2000). *Orientalism: A reader*. New York: New York University Press. Retrieved September 26, 2011, from Google Books.

Scholarly Article in Print Journal

Thompson, J. (2011). Magic for a people trained in pragmatism: Kenneth Burke and the early 9/11 Oratory of George W. Bush. *Rhetoric Review, 30,* 350–371.

Scholarly Article Found in Online Database

Angel, R. J. (2010). Immigrants and welfare: The impact of welfare reform on America's newcomers. *Contemporary Sociology: A Journal of Reviews, 39,* 568–569. Retrieved from http://csx.sagepub.com

Note: APA does not require that you list the database where you obtained an article unless the article would be difficult to locate.

Include the DOI, if available, or the url for the journal's homepage: Retrieved from http://csx.sagepub.com

Scholarly Article from Journal Published Online

Gustafsson, A. (2010). Beware the invisible. *Papers from the Institute of Archeology, 20.* doi:10.5334/pia.343

Note: This citation includes a doi (digital object identifier), which provides a permanent way to locate an article, even if databases or websites change.

Book Review

Schneider, R. J. (2004). [Review of the book *Modern physics and ancient faith*]. *Anglican Theological Review, 86,* 506–07.

Book Review Published Online

Garner, D. (2011, September 27). An unearthed treasure that changed things [Review of *The Swerve: How the world became modern*]. *The New York Times.* Retrieved from *www.nytimes.com*

An Editorial

Wolfe, G. (2011). The operation of grace [Editorial]. *Image: A Journal of the Arts and Religion, 70,* 3–4.

An Editorial Published Online

U.S. House: Members are not as uncivil as they seem [Editorial]. (2011, September 28). *Nation Now.* Retrieved September 29, 2011, from http://latimesblogs.latimes.com/nationnow/2011/09/us-house -more-civil-than-the-mid-90s-but-trouble-could-lay-ahead-.html

Note: This editorial was published in a blog called *Nation Now* that is published by the *Los Angeles Times*.

Magazine Article

Perry, A. (2011, September 26). Epidemic on the run. *Time*, 46–49.

Magazine Article from Online Database

Neuwirth, R. (2011, September). Global bazaar: Shantytowns, favelas and jhopadpattis turn out to be places of surprising innovation. *Scientific American*, 56–63. doi:10.1038/scientificamerican0911-56

Note: APA does not require you to cite the database where you obtained the article unless you think the article would be difficult to find.

Online Magazine Article

Leonard, A. (2011, September 29). A growing underworld bazaar. *Salon*. Retrieved, from http://www.salon.com/news/inside_the_shadow_economy/?story=/politics/feature/2011/09/29/shadowintro

Published Interview

Samantha Stosur, U.S. Open Champion [Interview by C. Murnieks]. (2011, September 23). In *Time*. Retrieved September 29, 2011, from http://www.time.com/time/arts/article/0,8599,2094349,00.html

Online Speech

King, Jr., M. L. (1963, August 28). *I have a dream*. Speech presented at March on Washington for Jobs and Freedom at the Lincoln Memorial, Washington, D.C. Retrieved September 29, 2011. Retrieved from http://www.americanrhetoric.com/speeches/mlkihaveadream.htm

Page on a Website

Coe, J. (2011, August 3). How to refinish a dresser. *How To*. Retrieved September 29, 2011, from http://www.sheknows.com/home-and-gardening/articles/837629/how-to-refinish-a-dresser

Image from a Website

Van Gogh, V. (1889). *Cypresses* [Online image]. Retrieved from http://www.metmuseum.org/toah/works-of-art/49.30

Blog Posting

Respect your audience [Web log post]. (2009). Retrieved September 15, 2011, from http://www.writersblock.ca/tips/monthtip/tipjan98.htm

Government Document

El Chamizal dispute: Compliance with convention of the Chamizal. (1964). *U.S. Senate Hearing.* Cleofas Calleros Papers. University of Texas at El Paso Library Special Collections (#33–9).

Government Document Online

Travis, W. B. (2005). *Letter from the Alamo, 1836.* Retrieved from Texas State Library & Archives Commission website: http//www.tslstate.tx.us/treasures/republic/Alamo/travis01.gov

Film

Coen, E. & Coen, J. (Producers and directors). (2007). *No country for old men* [Motion picture]. United States: Paramount Vantage.

DVD

Coen, E. & Coen, J. (Producers and directors). (2007). *No country for old men* [DVD]. United States: Paramount Vantage.

Television Program

Martin, D. (Reporter). (2008, March 2). The Pentagon's ray gun [Television series episode]. In M. Walsh (Producer) *60 Minutes*. New York, New York: CBS.

APA Parenthetical or (In-Text) Documentation

Direct Quote (shorter than 40 words)

"Scientists estimate that the rangewide population of the San Joaquin kit fox prior to 1930 was 8,000" (Conover, 2001, p. 44).

Direct Quote (40 words or longer)

Conover's 2001 study of the San Joaquin kit fox found the following:

> For the most part, in the "real" world kit foxes escape their preda-
> tors and the high temperatures of their desert environment by
> spending the day underground in a den. In Bakersfield, they follow
> suit. Kit foxes move every couple of weeks to a new den. Moving
> to different dens may be one reason why they have persisted; the
> constantly changing abodes provided new places to hide. (p. 199)
>
> **Note**: For a direct quote that exceeds 40 words, indent the pas-
> sage one-half inch from the left margin and set as a block, as
> shown here.

Direct Quote When the Author Is Named in the Text

Hildebrand (2004) stated that "generals of Alexander the Great brought news to Europe of vegetable wool which grew in tufts of trees in India" (p. 144).

Information from Printed Source (but not a direct quote)

It is common to see an Osprey make its nest on an electric power pole (Askew, 2002, p. 34).

Naming the Author of a Reference in Your Text, but Not Using a Direct Quote

Thompson (2002) maintained that . . .

In 2002, Thompson discovered . . .

Electronic or Other Sources Missing Author, Date, or Page Numbers

If your source provides section notations or paragraph numbers, indicate those. Use the paragraph ¶ symbol or the abbreviation para. and number.

(Bussell, 2000, ¶ 9)

If you include a quote from a text that has neither page numbers nor paragraph or section numbers, then the in-text citation should include a section heading (shortened if necessary) and the word "section" in place of the page number:

(Bussell, 2000, Introduction section).

If there is no author, as in an editorial, then give part of the name of the text and the date:

("Respect Your Audience," 2009).

If there is no date, then use n.d. If you have no date, no page number, and no author, your in-text citation will look as follows:

("The Future of Space," n.d.)

[23]

SAMPLE STUDENT PAPER IN APA FORMAT

Comment [LO3]: A shortened version of the title appears in the header of every page along with the page number.

Comment [LO1]: The phrase "Running head" appears on only the first page of the paper.

Anxiety and Memory: The Moderation Effect of Interviewing

Context on Children's Memory.

Taryn M. Coetzee

Oakland University

Comment [LO2]: The title page should include the title of the paper, the student's name, and the name of the university. All of this information is centered on the page in regular (not bolded or underlined) type.

Abstract

An abundance of research has been conducted in relation to child eyewitness testimony; however, the influence of interviewing context, for example, courtroom versus individual room, seems to be commonly overlooked. A review of research into the influencing factors on the reliability and accuracy of children's memory during testimony indicates a variety of influences, for example, questioning techniques and normative developmental factors. Particularly pertaining to the present study, the influence of interviewing context on anxiety, and, furthermore, the effects of increased levels of anxiety on children's memory, suggest an overall relationship between interviewing context and memory.

Comment [LO4]: The paper's abstract should appear on a separate page. The heading, "Abstract" is centered, but not bolded or underlined.

Anxiety and Memory: The Moderation Effect of Interviewing Context on Children's Memory

Children around the world may be required to testify in court for a number of reasons. For example, children may be exposed to criminal acts against themselves, witness criminal activity or even take part in criminal activity, all of which could lead to them testifying as eyewitnesses. Society generally perceives children to be vulnerable, innocent and even ignorant (Carpenter, 2005), a description that seems inappropriate when describing individuals who have been, and will be allowed to influence legal systems and help determine the fate of other people. Considering the seriousness of this issue, there is great importance in optimizing children's testimony by understanding the factors that may cause inaccurate and unreliable testimonies. Previous researchers have considered the accuracy and reliability of child eyewitness testimony from a variety of perspectives, primarily considering interviewing techniques and normative developmental factors like memory and cognition (Gross, 2005; Quas, Goodman, Ghetti, & Redlich, 2000). There does however, seem to be a gap in the research, where there has been little consideration of the effect of interviewing context, which could ultimately have a positive or negative influence on children and therefore on the outcomes of judiciary decisions. The current study examines previous research regarding the effect of interviewing context on children's level of anxiety, and, in turn the effect of increased anxiety on children's memory, which could ultimately infer a relationship between interviewing context and children's memory. Before considering the relationships between interviewing context, anxiety and memory, the previous research perspectives mentioned above must be taken into account.

Comment [LO5]: The paper's title is repeated above the introduction. It is centered on the page.

Comment [LO6]: The actual paper begins on a new page. The first sentence of each paragraph is indented 5 pts. The entire paper is double-spaced with Times New Roman, 12pt font (unless otherwise recommended by your instructor), with one inch margins all around.

EFFECTS OF INTERVIEWING CONTEXT ON MEMORY   4

Previous Research

Questioning Techniques

Verbal interviews. Questioning techniques play a role in determining the

accuracy of children's recollection as well as their level of susceptibility to suggestion

(Krackow, & Lynn, 2010; Lehman, Mckinley, Thompson, Leonard, Liebman, &

Rothrock, 2010). For example, Verkampt and Ginet (2010) examined the effectiveness

of the Cognitive Interview (CI) compared to the Structured Interview (SI) in very

young children, aged 4–5 years old and older children, aged 8–9 years old.

Comment [LO7]: A first-level heading is centered and bolded.

Comment [LO8]: A second-level heading is aligned left and bolded.

Comment [LO9]: A third-level heading is indented, bolded, and ends with a period. The first paragraph associated with this heading begins immediately after the period. Note that only the first word is capitalized with this heading.

EFFECTS OF INTERVIEWING CONTEXT ON MEMORY 5

References

Baron, R. M., & Kenny, D. A. (1986). The moderator-mediator variable distinction in

social psychological research: Conceptual, strategic, and statistical considerations.

Journal of Personality and Social Psychology, 51, 1173-1182. doi. 10.1037/0022-

3514.51.6.1173

Beidel, D. C. (1988). Psychophysiological assessment of anxious emotional stress in

children. *Journal of Abnormal Psychology, 97*, 80-82. doi: 10.1037/0021-

843X.97.1.80.

Carpenter, R. C. (2005). Women, children and other vulnerable groups: Gender, strategic

frames and the protection of civilians as a transnational issue. *International*

Studies Quarterly, 49, 295-334. doi: 10.1111/j.0020-8833.2005.00346.x.

Gross, R. (2005). *Psychology: The science of mind and behavior* (5th ed.). Tonbridge,

Kent: GreenGate Publishing Services.

Krackow, E. & Lynn, S. J. (2010). Event report training: An examination of the efficacy

of a new intervention to improve children's eyewitness reports. *Applied Cognitive*

Psychology, 24, 868-884. doi: 10.1002/acp.1594.

Lehman, E. B., Mckinley, M. J., Thompson, D. W., Leonard, A. M., Liebman, J. L. &

Rothrock, D. D. (2010). Long-term stability of young children's eyewitness

accuracy, suggestibility, and resistance to misinformation. *Journal of Applied*

Developmental Psychology, 31, 145-154. doi: 10.1016/j.appdev.2009.11.007

Nathanson, R. & Saywitz, K. (2003). The effects of the courtroom context on children's

memory and anxiety. *Journal of Psychiatry and Law, 31*, 67-98. Retrieved from

http://www.heinonline.org/HOL/CSV.csv?index=journals&collection=journals

Comment [LO11]: References begin on a new page and are double spaced.

Comment [LO12]: If a DOI number is available, use it for both print and online articles. If one is not available for an online article, include the permanent link to thet article.

Comment [LO13]: A book in its fifth edition

Comment [LO14]: If no DOI number is available, include the address for the permanent link to the article.

ABOUT THE CHAPTER AUTHORS

Ben Bennett-Carpenter is a Special Lecturer in the Department of Writing and Rhetoric and in the Bachelor of Liberal Studies program at Oakland University. He has published in several academic journals including the *Michigan Academician*, the *Journal of Communication and Religion*, and the journal *Mortality: Promoting the Interdisciplinary Study of Death and Dying*. He has served in a number of capacities at OU and serves as co-chair for the Interdisciplinary Studies section of the Michigan Academy of Science, Arts and Letters.

Marilyn Borner is a Writing and Rhetoric Department Special Lecturer. She has been with the university since 2007 and has served on the "Making Savvy Readers" Faculty Learning Committee and the Writing About Writing research team. She has served as the Writing & Rhetoric Department's webmaster. Publisher of *The Italian Tribune*, a bi-weekly newspaper serving Metro-Detroit since 1909, she also co-authored and edited the *Madison Heights Heritage Book II*. Previously, she was an editor and team leader for the *Orange County Register*, a daily newspaper in California, and an editor for the *Journal Advocate*, a daily newspaper in Sterling, Colorado.

Jill McKay Chrobak is a Special Lecturer in the Department of Writing and Rhetoric at Oakland University. She earned her Ph.D. in Writing and Rhetoric from Michigan State University in 2007 and is passionate about using Hip Hop, cultural rhetorics and other non-traditional texts in her composition pedagogy to foster a socially conscious writing community in her classroom. Jill is incredibly grateful to be able to teach writing to diverse, interesting and engaging students every semester.

Colleen Doyle earned her BA in English literature from Michigan State University and MA in Written Communication from Eastern Michigan University. She has been a journalist and promotional writer in the fields of business and non-profits.

Dana Lynn Driscoll's research interests include research methodologies, assessment, and writing centers. Her work has been published in *Across the Disciplines, Composition Forum, Computers and Composition,* and *WPA: Writing Program Administration* among other places.

Laura Gabrion has taught writing and literature at a variety of levels, and her specific interest is teaching writing with new media. She is a Teacher Consultant for the Meadow Brook Writing Project, coordinator of professional development activities, and a facilitator in the Meadow Brook Writing Project Youth Writing Camps at Meadow Brook Hall. Laura has been teaching at Oakland University since 2007, and she has built a rich environment in her classrooms by using a diverse set of instructional approaches.

Christina Hall has taught writing to students of all ages, and continues to teach writing workshops and celebrations to students in grades K-8, but her greatest passion lies in teaching first year writing at the university level. Some of her particular interests are metacognition, service learning, and videos composition. She has presented at local and national conferences on metacognition and reflection letters, as well as video use in the classroom. When she isn't teaching writing, she spends time outdoors with her son.

D.R. Hammontree serves as associate director of the first-year writing program. He teaches courses in first-year writing, business writing, global rhetorics, and peer tutoring in composition. He is a past president of the Michigan Council of Teachers of English.

Alice Horning is a former Professor of Writing and Rhetoric at Oakland University, where she holds a joint appointment in Linguistics. Her research over her entire career has focused on the intersection of reading and writing, focusing lately on the increasing evidence of students' reading difficulties and how to address them in writing courses and across the disciplines. Her work has appeared in the major professional journals and in books published by Parlor Press and Hampton Press. Her most recent book is *Reading, Writing, and Digitizing: Understanding Literacy in the Electronic Age* published in 2012 by Cambridge Scholars Publishing.

Jenna Katz is a Special Lecturer at Oakland University where she teaches Business Writing and Composition. Jenna has been a professional writer since 2002 and has been teaching writing, career readiness, and communication since 2008. With experience working in corporate, non-profit, and academic environments, Jenna is able to help students develop and communicate their ideas in college and in their careers. She holds a Bachelor of Arts in Humanities from Michigan State University and a Master of Arts in Writing from DePaul University.

Christina Moore is a Special Lecturer at Oakland University. Her master's work in English explored writing genres less-privileged classes used to inject their voice into mass media. Her study of the epistolary genre in the Harlem Renaissance has been accepted for publication in the African American Review. In response to the shift from print genres to digital genres, Christina currently studies new media influence on student self-perception of writing, specifically social media and mobile devices. Her classes follow a project-based model that applies academic writing to practical purposes and local audiences.

Lori Ostergaard is the Chair of the Department of Writing and Rhetoric and an Associate Professor whose archival research examines the history of composition-rhetoric at Midwestern normal schools and high schools. In addition to teaching First-Year Writing classes, she teaches classes in Peer Tutoring for Composition, Digital Storytelling, Digital Culture, Composition Studies, Teaching of Writing, and Teaching Writing with New Media.

Lauren E. Rinke has been teaching at Oakland University since 2010. In addition to teaching first year writing courses, she co-facilitates the fall and spring Writing Marathons, as well as the Meadow Brook Writing Project's summer youth writing workshops. As an OU alum and instructor, Rinke loves the community and atmosphere of Oakland. She achieves to foster within her students the ability to communicate and write conscientiously and coherently, in order to maintain successful academic and professional careers, and hopefully affect positive change in the world.

ABOUT THE STUDENT AUTHORS

Taryn Coetzee, an international transfer student at Oakland University, is a senior majoring in Psychology and planning to attend graduate school to complete a PhD. Taryn is a writing consultant at the Oakland University Writing Center, and furthermore, a research assistant within the Psychology department. Taryn enjoys the challenge and opportunity for critical thinking and research that accompanies the task of writing research papers. The presented literature review, which appears as the APA sample paper, was written for Dr. Mary Lewis' PSY 321: Child Development class. The guidance from Dr. Lewis, and peers, was enormously instrumental throughout the writing and research process of the literature review.

Caitlin Keech is a first-year student at Oakland University who is majoring in Political Science. Her essay was written for her WRT 150: Composition I class in the Fall of 2015. The subject matter was inspired by her dream to be a photojournalist and her curiosity about the rhetoric involved in the field. She is extremely grateful for her teacher, Professor Melissa St. Pierre, who encouraged her and taught her that she could be a good writer.

Elizabeth Kellogg is a junior Sociology major, with interests in social stratification and environmental sociology. Her research for this essay was done for Professor Laura Klein's WRT 160: Composition II class. She credits Professor Klein for motivating her and helping her finish her research by providing supportive feedback. Kellogg chose to write on prison rehabilitation programs because she feels that prisoners are an often-maligned group who deserve further discussion and review about their treatment while incarcerated. She plans on becoming a civil rights attorney and will use the research strategies she learned while preparing this paper in her future work, both academically and professionally.

Anthony Polito is a senior at OU who is completing his work for his major in Computer Science. His research and essay were completed for Professor Laura Gabrion's WRT 160: Composition II class. Polito's research for this essay was inspired by a passion for technological progress and fighting scientific misinformation.

Emily Stamper is a first-year student at OU pursuing an English Degree from the College of Arts and Sciences. This essay was a reflection on WRT 160: Composition II class, taught by Professor Crystal VanKooten. Stamper's essay was inspired by her experiences in the class, both in refining her writing and learning how to make a rhetorical video. She is thankful for the help and support she received from her professor and for the constructive criticism from her classmates.

APPENDIX A: FIRST-YEAR WRITING CLASS DESCRIPTIONS

The Department of Writing and Rhetoric offers first-year writing classes that focus on helping students to develop the rhetorical skills, processes, and information literacies necessary for writing and composing in the 21st century. Our classes focus on community and civic engagement, new media composition, collaborative writing, and revision.

WRT 102: Basic Writing

Students in **WRT 102, Basic Writing** will work with both a First-Year Writing instructor and an embedded tutor from the University's Writing Center to develop their writing skills, including idea generation and invention, organizational strategies, and conventional usage in expository prose.

In WRT 102, Basic Writing, you will learn to

- approach writing as a multi-step, recursive process that requires feedback
- compose your texts to address the rhetorical situation
- demonstrate an ability to synthesize information/ideas in and between various texts—written, spoken, and visual
- reflect on your own writing processes and evaluate your own learning
- adapt your prior knowledge and learning strategies to a variety of new writing and reading situations in college and beyond
- develop the habits of mind of effective college writers and readers.

WRT 150: Composition I

Students in **WRT 150, Composition I** are introduced to the rhetorical and stylistic demands of college writing through a focus on experiential, analytical, and expressive writing. Students in Composition I learn to generate, organize and develop their ideas and to make choices as writers that are appropriate to the rhetorical situation.

In WRT 150, Composition I, you will learn to

- Analyze rhetorical situations (writer, text, context, purpose, audience) in a variety of genres and media.

- Define and enact appropriate rhetorical strategies, including kairos, ethos, logos, pathos, to communicate ideas in a variety of genres.

- Apply rhetorical knowledge to gain a better understanding of a professional discourse community.

- Develop strategies for reading rhetorically, evaluating, and responding to a variety of texts, including visual, electronic, written and verbal texts.

- Reflect on their own writing processes, evaluate their own learning, transfer and adapt their learning to new settings, and develop the habits of mind of effective college writers.

- Employ writing as a process of making meaning, requiring multiple drafts and revision.

- Demonstrate syntactic fluency and control of language conventions, including awareness of sentence and paragraph structure.

- Exhibit accurate use of and rhetorical purpose for documentation systems, generally MLA.

WRT 160: Composition II

Students in **WRT 160, Composition II** classes are exposed to methods of research and writing including the use of rhetorical strategies and synthesis of scholarly sources to create academic arguments. This class emphasizes processes of writing and revision with a focus on information literacy, critical thinking, and effective communication in diverse rhetorical contexts. The successful completion of WRT 160, Composition II with a 2.0 or higher satisfies the university general education requirement in the writing knowledge foundation area.

In WRT 160, Composition II, you will learn

- primary research methods (quantitative and qualitative) appropriate for academic scholarship
- secondary research strategies for locating and evaluating sources both through library databases and through external online databases appropriate for academic scholarship
- ethical considerations in academic scholarship, including responsibility to human subjects, non-biased use of language, fair and accurate use of sources, appropriate documentation, and larger rhetorical purposes of civic engagement
- stylistic conventions for integrating secondary and primary research to arrive at new knowledge in academic disciplines, including familiarity with APA format

In this course, you will also

- make connections with the broader community through activities related to civic and community engagement on and/or off campus
- demonstrate familiarity with basic rhetorical, ethical, and methodological conventions of academic disciplines (such as humanities, sciences, social sciences) to prepare them for further study in their chosen discipline
- demonstrate the ability to locate and analyze scholarly sources critically and synthesize them to produce various academic genres which include print, visual, digital, or oral elements

Because WRT 160, Composition II, is the writing foundation requirement, the course also meets a number of general education learning outcomes and cross-cutting capacities.

General Education Learning Outcomes

The writing knowledge foundation area prepares students to demonstrate:

- knowledge of the elements, writing processes and organizing strategies for creating analytical and expository prose
- effective rhetorical strategies appropriate to the topic, audience, context and purpose

Cross-Cutting Capacities

- effective communication
- critical thinking
- information literacy

WRT 104, Supervised Study

Students who want additional help with their writing in any of our introductory writing courses or in any of the university's writing-intensive courses may elect to enroll in **WRT 104, Supervised Study**. This 1-2 credit course provides students with tutorial instruction from a WRT faculty member based on the areas of writing the student wishes to work on. Students who take WRT 104 unanimously praise this course for the one-on-one time the course provides and the assistance our WRT 104 instructors offer for writing assignments in a variety of classes. For example, a WRT 104 student from fall 2011 praised his course instructor because she "thoroughly walked through every assignment with me," and another applauded the instructor's ability to teach "in different styles until we found the one best fit for my learning." Our research also indicates that students with low ACT scores who enroll in WRT 104 generally have higher pass rates in WRT 160 than students who choose not to enroll in this course.

In WRT 104, Supervised Study, you will learn to

- interpret the rhetorical situation (audience, context, purpose) that a writing assignment asks students to address
- identify the requirements of a specific writing assignment

- use a variety of techniques to generate ideas and to draft, organize, revise, edit, and reflect on their writing

- recognize and correct patterns of error in standard edited English that interfere with or distort meaning

- produce academic prose that demonstrates an understanding of college-level argumentation (or other course-specific writing tasks)

OU students are also required to complete at least one Writing-Intensive course in their majors and one Writing-Intensive course outside of their majors as a part of their general education requirements. In addition to offering both a major and a minor in Writing and Rhetoric (Appendix G), our department offers a number of upper-level Writing-Intensive courses for non-majors.

APPENDIX B: UNIVERSITY AND DEPARTMENT POLICIES

First-Year Writing Placement Policies

Most students will begin their college writing experience by taking Composition I (WRT 150) and Composition II (WRT 160). Some students may be recommended to take WRT 104 (Supervised Study) based on early writing samples in their classes.

To fulfill Oakland University's general education writing foundations requirement, students must complete WRT 160 or its equivalent with a 2.0 or higher. Ideally, students should complete their writing foundations requirement (WRT 160) before their junior year and before they take their Writing Intensive in General Education courses. As with any other unfulfilled general education course, transferring juniors and seniors who have not completed writing foundations should do so immediately.

Students with questions about placement (https://wwwp.oakland.edu/fyac/courseplacement/) in first year writing should consult the Department of Writing and Rhetoric, 378 O'Dowd Hall, 248-370-2746, prior to the beginning of the semester in which they plan to enroll in first year writing.

OU Excused Absence Policy and WRT Department Attendance Policy

All WRT classes adhere to the OU Excused Absence Policy (https://wwwp.oakland.edu/provost/policies-and-procedures/) for OU events and activities. For absences not covered by the university policy, students in writing and rhetoric courses are allowed a certain number of absences without penalty: 3 for MWF classes, 2 for TR classes, or 1 for evening classes. This includes absences due to illness, car trouble, or schedule conflicts. Participation in online activities counts as class attendance. For each absence beyond those allowed, the student's final course grade will be lowered by 0.1 points on the 4.0 scale for MWF classes, .15 for TTh classes, or .3 for evening and Saturday classes. Students who miss *more than* three combined weeks of class are not eligible to receive a grade above 0.0.

Faculty Feedback

Faculty Feedback is a system for providing feedback to students who may be falling behind in a course. If you receive faculty feedback suggesting that your instructor is concerned about your work in a Writing and Rhetoric class, make an appointment to meet with your instructor outside of class time to review your work and discuss some strategies for improving your performance in the class.

Incompletes

Incompletes can only be given if circumstances beyond the control of the student occur after the official withdrawal date and preclude timely completion of the work for a course. Student and instructor must agree on the terms under which the work will be completed and evaluated, and should complete and sign the University Registrar's form available for this purpose. The form is available from the Writing and Rhetoric Department office (378 O'Dowd Hall) and from the Registrar's office (100 O'Dowd Hall).

Adds/Drops

All WRT classes adhere to the university policy on adds, drops, and withdrawals (https://wwwp.oakland.edu/provost/policies-and-procedures/). It is your responsibility to be aware of the University deadline dates for dropping out of any WRT course.

You are also responsible for knowing registration deadlines and understanding the implications of schedule changes on your financial aid. Because we cannot possibly manage the schedules of thousands of students every year, the WRT department is not responsible for your loss of financial aid due to schedule changes, so be sure to check with an advisor and with the financial aid office before you decide to drop any class at the university. You may add or drop WRT classes using SAIL during open enrollment periods.

Because smaller class sizes allow for more instructor feedback on your work and more small group workshopping of papers, we keep our WRT classes capped at 22 students per section (18 students for WRT 102). WRT department policy will not permit faculty to over-enroll their classes for this reason. In addition, you may not add into WRT classes after SAIL registration closes. Because of the length of time that SAIL registration is available to students, WRT instructors are advised not to sign any add slips. The first two weeks of class cover important material and often include graded assignments. Enrollment after that cutoff would be unfair both to you and to the rest of the class.

Preferred Name and Pronoun Policy

If you do not identify with the name that is listed with the registrar, please notify your course instructor so that they may appropriately amend their records.

In addition, if you prefer to go by a different pronoun, please inform your instructor.

A Statement about Peer Review and Sharing Your Work

The grades you earn in your Writing and Rhetoric classes are confidential. However, the texts you produce in our classes will be shared with your classmates as a part of our regular peer review process. Our classes will prepare you to meet the needs of a variety of readers in college and beyond, and to do so, we provide ample opportunity for your compositions to be read and responded to by classmates and by the course instructor. You should, therefore, always assume that the work you compose in our classes is public, not private.

Student Grade Grievance Policy

Department policies may change from year to year, so students who are considering filing a grievance should contact the department for the most recent version of the policy outlined below.

The purpose of this statement is to set forth a procedure that will permit resolution of student complaints immediately after they arise and in the spirit of cooperation. All complaints must be initiated within sixty (60) days after the student is aware of the circumstances leading to the complaint. *This policy complies with the time limits set forth in the University Grievance Procedure.*

A student who has a complaint about a classroom situation involving an instructor teaching under the WRT rubric has, first, recourse to that instructor. Any member of the Department to whom the student makes his/her complaint must send that student directly to the instructor involved.

If the student and instructor are unable to resolve differences themselves, or if the student finds it impossible to meet with the instructor directly, the student should take his/her *written complaint* to the Chair of the department. The criteria for the grounds of a grievance shall include evidence of:

- systematic and demonstrable unfairness based on ethnicity, race, or gender (complaints of discrimination will be forwarded to the dean of students office)

- inconsistent application of instructor's grading policy (i.e. how the final grade is derived)
- inconsistent application of standards established by the instructor (i.e. clearly differing evaluation criteria brought into play from student to student in the same assignment)
- inconsistent course procedures relative to those laid out in the syllabus.

Complaints of grading harshness or professional evaluation by instructors of classroom presentations or written essays do not constitute sufficient grounds unless clear evidence of above criteria is present.

Upon receipt of the formal written grievance, the Department Chair or the Chair of the Grievance Committee will hold an informal meeting with the student and instructor (individually or together as deemed appropriate) in an effort to reach a mutually agreeable solution to the grievance.

If the informal arbitration between the Department Chair or Chair of the Grievance Committee (CGC), student and instructor does not resolve the issue, the CGC and the WRT Chair or designated full-time WRT faculty member will review the complaint to determine whether or not it meets the criteria stated above. If it does not, the WRT Chair will inform the student and the process will conclude.

If it is determined the complaint meets the criteria, CGC will form an arbitration panel consisting of three (3) people from the university community including: the CGC, one chosen by the student, one by the instructor.

The mediation panel will hold a hearing in the presence of both parties. After the meeting the panel will confer in closed session to discuss potential remedies, if deemed appropriate. The panel will provide the instructor with recommendations for addressing the grievance or will inform the student that the grievance was without merit. If the Chair deems there are not grounds for the grievance based on the criteria above, the student will be informed and the process will be concluded.

If the student is not satisfied by the arbitration process, she/he may then contact the office of the Dean of the College of Arts and Sciences to pursue a grievance at the College level.

In the case of grading complaints, the panel can suggest the instructor reevaluate the student's work (which might result in raising or lowering the grade), but the panel does not have the power to change grades. Although collegial recommendation carries positive weight, ultimately the teacher of record decides the final grade. For other classroom situations, the panel can likewise recommend a resolution, but, ultimately, the instructor of record controls his/her classroom. The suggestion of the panel shall be the final stage of the departmental action.

Faculty members are also to be guided by the statements on faculty conduct and professionalism contained in the Faculty Agreement. In addition, it should be noted that non-academic concerns, discrimination, and harassment complaints are governed by the *Oakland University Procedure for the Resolution of Student Complaints*.

Academic Conduct Regulations

Cheating on examinations, plagiarism, falsifying reports/records, and unauthorized collaboration, access, or modifying of computer programs are considered serious breaches of academic conduct. The Oakland University policy on academic conduct will be strictly followed with no exceptions. See catalog under Academic Policies and Procedures.

If upon reviewing a student project, an instructor suspects that a student has engaged in plagiarism, the instructor will issue an incomplete on the assignment and forward the matter with a letter of explanation and supporting documentation to the Office of the Dean of Students. The instructor will indicate clearly the passages that s/he believes are plagiarized and provide the Dean of Students with their original source if possible. Once the matter is resolved by the Academic Conduct Committee, the faculty member will issue the appropriate grade on the assignment. If an Incomplete has been issued for the final grade, the instructor will complete a change of grade form as appropriate, and under the reason for change of grade, note, "Final grade due to resolution of academic conduct matter."

Additional information about OU's Academic Conduct Regulations is available in the OU Student Handbook (http://catalog.oakland.edu/content.php?catoid=14&navoid=700).

APPENDIX C: ONLINE CLASS EXPECTATIONS

Moodle is an interactive and engaging part of students' experiences in all of our first-year writing classes. One week before classes begin, you may login to Moodle to find your instructor contact information, the course syllabus, the course calendar, and other course materials. Your instructor may use Moodle to post course assignments, handouts, resources, reading assignments, feedback, links, videos, audio lectures, PowerPoint presentations, and course grades. All online communication between you and your course instructor will occur through *Moodle* or *OU Webmail*.

Partially-Online Classes

All of OU's writing classes are listed as *Partially Online*, and may include anywhere from 10% to 30% of online course activities, depending on your instructor. During the semester, you may interact with your classmates and your instructor beyond the classroom walls by logging in to Moodle for readings, forum postings, wiki development, research activities, group work, peer reviews, and multimedia projects as part of your required work for the class.

All first-year writing courses (WRT 102, WRT 150, and WRT 160) are designated as partially-online. This means that if you've registered for a Tuesday/Thursday, Monday/Wednesday/Friday, or evening course, your class will meet in the classroom for the majority of the time, but you may occasionally be asked to participate in an online class. Your online class time will involve some kind of interactive assignment in Moodle, with a deadline for completing this work that will be determined by your course instructor. These interactive online assignments count as part of your course attendance and participation, and failure to complete online work by the deadline may seriously damage your course grade.

Online Classes

Courses listed as *Online* in SAIL may have up to 3 optional on campus meetings, but all graded coursework for fully online classes takes place in Moodle. If you are enrolled in an online writing class, you should be prepared to check Moodle on the first day of classes, log in several times each week, and check your OU Webmail accounts daily for instructions from your online course instructor. Fully online classes can be very challenging for students who have trouble self-motivating because they require students to take an active role in their own learning. Rather than attend class where the required information is presented to the class by the course instructor, online students must access and understand the required information on their own. The withdraw and failure rates for online classes are much higher than for partially-online classes for this reason.

Succeeding in the Online Class Environment

Success in partially- and fully-online writing classes at OU depends almost entirely on your ability to keep up with course readings and assignments and on your ability to meet deadlines for completing online course activities. The OU Student Catalog states that the standard Oakland University course is a 4-credit course which is scheduled for 200 minutes (3 hours and 20 minutes) per week of "seat time." For online and partially-online classes, work in Moodle generally counts as seat time. Also, for every one hour of seat time, there are generally two hours of preparation—reading texts, reviewing materials and notes, fieldwork, and writing. In total, you can expect to spend 10 hours per week on each 4 credit—online, partially-online, or face-to-face—WRT course you take. During summer semesters, that time commitment is doubled.

If you are enrolled in a MWF class and your instructor has told you that your class will be meeting online rather in the classroom, you will be expected to complete online "seat time" activities that would be equivalent to the time you would have spent in class on that day (67 minutes). If your Tuesday/Thursday partially-online class meets online for one class period, you should expect to spend the equivalent of 107 minutes completing online assignments. And if your once-a-week evening class meets online rather than on campus any week, you should expect to spend about 200 minutes completing online work for that week. These estimates for the amount of time you should spend completing online class "seat time" activities do not include the time you should also spend completing homework assignments or readings.

Successful participants in partially- or fully-online classes check into Moodle regularly throughout the week to find out what will be expected of them that week and when their online work will need to be completed. These students enter the online class space prepared to engage actively and purposefully with course material and to contribute critical and insightful responses to on-line class discussions. Students who have the most success in our online and partially-online classes understand that the technology may let them down from time to time, so they don't wait until the last minute to submit work or participate in online discussions.

APPENDIX D: A GLOSSARY OF TERMS FOR USE IN FIRST-YEAR WRITING CLASSES

Analysis — a Greek term (*analusis*), which translates as "to loosen" or "to unbind." Analysis defines the process of breaking a complex topic into smaller parts so that topic may be easier to understand and explain.

Argument — used as a persuasive tool, written arguments begin with a claim that is clearly constructed as well as arguable in nature. The claim is supported by logical evidence and the argument may include a consideration (and refutation) of the opposing viewpoints.

Audience — The readers, consumers, or end users you hope to reach with your communication. Various kinds of audiences are often present for each rhetorical situation including primary audiences (who you are directly writing to) and secondary audiences (related others who may read your work). Often, it is wise for writers beginning a new writing task or entering a new rhetorical situation to perform an audience analysis to determine what the audience values, believes, respects, feels, etc.

Collaboration — Working together to reach a common goal. Collaborative efforts in the writing classroom often involve sharing elements of research responsibilities as well as sharing the workload involved in a writing project. As opposed to thinking of these tasks as atomized and discreet though, with everyone in the group taking on a single part in the project, WRT instructors prefer more thorough involvement in each step of the process from every individual in the group, as well as frequent peer reviews to locate areas for improvement and collaborative revision and editing.

Composition — Composition involves any creative act that culminates in a textual product. It is the process of writing writ large to include hypertext, filmic text, photographic text, as well as more traditional alphabetical text.

Furthermore, composition refers to a discipline that applies rhetorical principles, especially notions of audience and purpose, to the creation of textual objects. Composition also encompasses the rhetorical study of textual objects.

Discourse Community — a social or professional group (such as a classroom, a department, a discipline, an organization, a company, or an online community) where writing takes place.

Ethnography — a Greek term, which translates as *ethnos* "folk, people" and *grapho* "to write." Ethnography is a type of qualitative research that involves detailed, thick descriptions of everyday life, and usually lends itself to studying a group of people or a cultural practice in depth. Field notes, observations and thick descriptions of those observations, participant-observation, and the collection of artifacts are methods used in ethnographic work. Although ethnography originated in the field of anthropology, it is now widely used as a method of understanding cultural phenomenon in many fields, including in writing and rhetoric.

Ethos — a Greek term that translates, roughly, as the writer's authority, credibility, or character. Your audience will be more willing to listen to you, will be more likely to be moved or persuaded by your text, if you come across as a "good [person] speaking well" (Quintilian 12.1.1).

Incorporation (of sources) — the process in academic writing that requires the insertion of information from outside sources. This information may be included in a text to introduce a new concept, support a claim, illustrate a point, review previous research, etc. When writers incorporate other sources of information into their own texts, they typically introduce each new source, briefly summarizing the source and identifying the author and title of the work; quote or paraphrase a relevant passage from the work; and explain how this source relates to their own work (as a support, counter-argument, illustration, etc.).

Informed Consent — a term used within primary research to describe the process of ensuring that human participants understand and consent to the nature of a research study, the risks involved, what they gain by participating, and the fact that they are free to withdraw their participation. With professional research studies, this often involves an informed consent form that outlines these principles and asks for a participant's signature.

Interview — a meeting or conversation in which a writer or reporter asks prepared questions of one or more persons from whom information is sought. This information will then be used in an academic essay, newspaper story, television broadcast, etc.

Kairos — the Greek term rhetors use to mean "the opportune moment," the perfect moment for speaking (or acting) on a particular issue.

Logos — We get the word "logic" from the Greek word logos, and it signifies a claim that is based in fact or reason (rather than emotion or character). Statistics and survey data can be used as appeals to logic, as can claims supported by sound reasoning.

Metacognition — According to the *Framework for Success in Post-Secondary Writing*, metacognition refers to the "ability to reflect on one's own thinking." It is often referred to as "thinking about thinking" (Council of Writing Program Administrators, 2011, p. 1).

Multimodal — the word "multimodal" means to possess or use more than one mode to communicate. In writing courses, multimodal projects employ more than just one mode of communication to reach an audience. A multimodal project might combine written text and images, video and sound, spoken texts and a slide show, etc.

New Media — new media contrasts older, more static forms of media (i.e., books, articles) because it is digital, accessible and potentially interactive. New media has a direct impact on traditional composition studies because it allows students to persuade, inform, or entertain an audience using a variety of technologies and modalities.

Paraphrase — Purdue University's Online Writing Lab (OWL) suggests that paraphrase "involves putting a passage from source material into your own words. A paraphrase must also be attributed to the original source. Paraphrased material is usually shorter than the original passage, taking a somewhat broader segment of the source and condensing it slightly" ("Quoting, Paraphrasing and Summarizing," 2013, para. 4).

Pathos — the Greek term for the practice of using words (images, sounds, etc.) to sway an audience's emotions.

Peer Review — Peer review is a collaborative activity that involves writers reading each other's work and responding to that work rhetorically. This means going beyond simple line editing and, instead, discussing the contextual purpose of the piece, the rhetorical strategies the author has used to effectively carry out that purpose, and the strategies the author might add to the piece to make it more effective. Peer review can occur in person or in a digital format so long as it involves collaboration, discussion, and critical feedback.

Plagiarism — According to the Council of Writing Program Administrators (2003), "in an instructional setting, plagiarism occurs when a writer deliberately uses someone else's language, ideas, or other original (not common-knowledge) material without acknowledging its source" ("Defining and Avoiding Plagiarism," para. 4).

Portfolio — According to compositionist K. B. Yancey (2001), a portfolio is a compilation of writing that encompasses three activities by the student: collection, selection, and reflection. Yancey suggests that "student portfolios can be succinctly defined as collections of work selected from a larger archive of work, upon which the student has reflected" (p. 16).

Purpose — Effective rhetors take questions of rhetorical situation and audience into consideration at the outset of the writing process and apply those considerations at each step. We might think of purpose as tacitly posing the questions: "What are my goals as a writer? Whom am I trying to reach and to what end? Which rhetorical strategies might best help me achieve my purpose?"

Questionnaire or Survey — Surveys or questionnaires are short, usually close-ended data collection instruments used to gain small amounts of information from various people. Surveys are used to learn about a general trend in people's opinions, experiences, and behavior (Driscoll, 2011).

Reflection — Students in WRT courses are regularly required to compose reflections analyzing the work they are engaged in or completing in their class. Reflection supports learning by requiring that the learner take some time to think about and analyze what s/he has done, what lessons can be learned from the work, how the work might apply to other learning situations, how rhetoric and research informed the work, and what the writer might do differently next time.

Research, Primary — the research writers conduct themselves. In the sciences, primary research may take the form of experiments conducted in controlled, laboratory conditions or observations and experiments in the natural world. In the humanities and social sciences, primary research often engages with human subjects through ethnography or participant-observation, observations, interviews, or surveys. Primary research may also include an analysis of historical texts.

Research, Secondary — the gathering of other writers' published research to gain multiple perspectives on a topic and a variety of supports for claims and arguments. Credible secondary research is most often found in library databases, in academic journals, and in books.

Revision — A writer's attempt to improve a text or composition. Revision typically entails creating more than one draft and making holistic changes to the "global' issues in the texts. Global issues are those that deal with ideas or arguments. Revision entails re-envisioning the overall effectiveness of the composition. Revision is not proofreading or copyediting, as these two activities focus on "local," or smaller, issues such as grammar, spelling and punctuation.

Rhetoric — the study of the strategies for using language effectively to persuade, inform, or entertain an audience. Aristotle defined rhetoric as "the faculty of observing in any given case the available means of persuasion" (1.1.1355b25-6).

Rhetorical Analysis — a textual analysis focuses on the audience and purpose of a text and analyzes the rhetorical strategies (and effectiveness of those strategies) employed by the writer/speaker/composer/designer of that text.

Rhetorical Situation — the context for a rhetorical act. Effective writers and rhetors work to make themselves aware of the rhetorical context for their work, of the purpose of their work, of the situations and circumstances surrounding their topic, of the ways their work will be received by their audiences, of the rhetorical strategies that will work best with their particular audiences, and of the consequences of their joining a particular conversation.

Rhetorical Triangle – According to J.D. Nugent (2004), "the rhetorical triangle is a way of thinking about what's involved in any communication/persuasion scenario. It involves (no surprise here) three main parts" (para. 8). While there are a number of different rhetorical triangles depicting the rhetorical situation (some position ethos, pathos, and logos at each corner), the most common depicts rhetor/writer, audience/reader, and purpose at each corner (Nugent, 2004).

Sources — In academic research, information can be gathered from a variety of sources. Those sources may be individuals who participate in interviews, researchers publishing their work in academic journals, eyewitnesses to events, etc. When citing a particular source, it is important to consider that source's ethos by discerning whether or not your audience will consider the source to be credible, knowledgeable, trustworthy, unbiased, etc.

Summary — There are three ways writers usually weave information from other writers and researchers into their own compositions: quoting, paraphrasing and summarizing. According to the Purdue University Online Writing Lab (2013), "Summarizing involves putting the main idea(s) into your own words, including only the main point(s) [of a particular work.] Summaries are significantly shorter than the original and take a broad overview of the source material" ("Quoting, Paraphrasing and Summarizing," 2013, para. 5).

Synthesis — in its most basic form, synthesis is weaving together information found in several sources in order to generate new ideas. Synthesis also has its origins in Greece (*sunthesis*) and defines the act of "putting together" or combining.

Transfer of Learning — Transfer of learning is a term used to describe students' ability to apply and adapt knowledge from one context to another context. Transfer of learning includes understanding and encouraging students to use their prior knowledge in their current writing course (so using middle/high school writing experiences in FYW) and also encouraging students to anticipate and adapt their learning to new circumstances (such as taking what they learned in FYW and applying it to writing intensive courses).

Writing — typically viewed as the alphabetic composition of a writer's ideas to a specific audience and for a specific purpose, writing further incorporates the writer's use of a variety of rhetorical devices as well as the possible use of other forms of media in order to convey meaning.

References

Aristotle. (trans. 2007) *On rhetoric: A theory of civic discourse.* (G.A. Kennedy, trans., 2nd ed.) New York: Oxford UP.

Council of Writing Program Administrators. (2003). *Defining and Avoiding Plagiarism: The WPA Statement on Best Practices.* Retrieved from http://wpacouncil.org/positions/WPAplagiarism.pdf

Council of Writing Program Administrators, National Council of Teachers of English, & National Writing Project. (2011). *Framework for Success in Postsecondary Writing.* Retrieved from http://wpacouncil.org/framework.

Driscoll, D.L. (2011). Introduction to primary research: observations, surveys, and interviews. In C.L. Lowe & P. Zemliansky (Eds.), *Writing spaces: Readings on writing.* (Vol. 2). Retrieved from http://writingspaces.org/essays.

Nugent, J.D. (2004). About rhetoric. Retrieved from http://tech-rhet.net/resources/rhetoric/

Quintilian, M. F. (1951). The institutio oratorio of Marcus Fabius Quintilianus (C.E. Little, Trans.) Nashville, TN*: George Peabody College for Teachers.*

Quoting, paraphrasing, and summarizing. (2013). Purdue Online Writing Lab. Retrieved from https://owl.english.purdue.edu/owl/resource/563/01/

Yancey, K.B. (2001). Digitized student portfolios. In B.L. Cambridge (Ed.), *Electronic Portfolios: Emerging in student, faculty, and institutional learning.* Washington, D.C.: American Association for Higher Education. 15-30.

APPENDIX E: STUDENT SUPPORT AND RESOURCES

Your Writing and Rhetoric Instructor

Instructors in the Department of Writing and Rhetoric are experts in the field of Composition and Rhetoric who shape the work they do with our first-year students based on current research, theories, and best practices in the field. All Writing and Rhetoric faculty possess two or more advanced degrees in the field of Composition and Rhetoric, English, Professional Writing, or an associated field of study. Our faculty regularly enroll in additional graduate coursework in composition and pedagogy, engage in professional development workshops and activities, attend and present at national conferences in the field, and publish scholarship on writing instruction. Many of our course instructors are also involved in organizing and leading department activities like the Writing Excellence Awards and Writing Marathons; or in university or community activities like the Meadow Brook Writing Project, Youth Writing Camps and Youth Writing Half-Day Workshops, the Digital Archive of Literacy Narratives, and the Rochester Oral History Archive.

All of our instructors are deeply committed to helping you succeed in your writing classes at OU and beyond, so we encourage you to meet with your instructor outside of class to discuss your work throughout the semester. Writing and Rhetoric instructors are available during their scheduled office hours and by appointment to provide you with additional feedback on your writing; however, because WRT instructors also take part in meetings, workshops, and events around campus, you may not always find your instructor in his/her office if it is not his/her office hours or if you have not scheduled an appointment in advance.

One of the most important responsibilities your course instructor has is providing useful, constructive feedback to the work you and your classmates compose in our first-year writing classes. Quality feedback that addresses both the strengths and the weaknesses of a particular paper or project, and that proposes suggestions for revision, takes a lot of time and effort. For this reason, you can generally expect to receive your instructor's response to your papers within about two weeks after you've handed them in. While this response time may vary depending on the type of draft you submitted, the number of other drafts your instructor is responding to at the time, and the amount of course prep, committee work, or service obligations your instructor has, generally most of our first-year instructors are able to return papers to their students within two weeks.

Most WRT instructors share office phones, which means that messages left on your instructor's office phone may not be responded to immediately. Email is usually the best way to contact your instructor, but please plan ahead to allow at least 24 hours for a response to your emails, and 48 hours on weekends or over school holidays. Check your course syllabus to discover the best means for reaching your instructor, and be sure to make a note of your instructor's office hours, office location, and email address at the beginning of the semester.

Information about your class—the syllabus, course policies, and course schedule—is also available through your Moodle classroom, and many instructors post additional course materials to Moodle to assist you in completing required assignments.

The Writing Center (http://www.oakland.edu/ouwc)

The Oakland University Writing Center, located on the main floor of Kresge Library, offers an environment where students can openly communicate with peer and faculty writing consultants about all areas of the writing process. These services are available for all majors of study, and to all undergraduate and graduate students. Well-qualified, trained peer consultants can help you understand your assignments, generate ideas, organize your thoughts, develop your claims points, understand your audience and purpose, and revise and edit your project drafts.

The Student Technology Center (http://www.oakland.edu/stc)

The Student Technology Center (STC) is the headquarters for the promotion, instruction and support of technology literacy. From beginners looking to learn the basics to experts seeking to hone their skills, the STC's training, education and hands-on learning experiences offers on-campus services to meet OU students' ever-increasing technology needs. Core services include technology mentoring and free equipment loans. By aiding students in their academic and personal pursuits, the services available through the STC build and enhance technological skills that lead to success—in the classroom, workplace and life. The STC is located in the basement of the Oakland Center.

Disability Support Services (http://www.oakland.edu/dss)

Oakland University maintains an office to assist students with special needs. Advocacy and support services are provided through the Office of Disability Support Services located in 157 North Foundation Hall (248-370-3266, 3268 for TDD). Services include, but are not limited to, priority registration, special testing arrangements, assistive technology, referrals to outside service agencies, assistance in identifying volunteer notetakers and volunteer readers, assistance with sign language interpreter services and with any general needs or concerns. Students with special needs are encouraged to utilize these services. The University Diversity and Compliance office (148 North Foundation Hall, 248-370-3496) is also available to assist students with disabilities.

The Graham Counseling Center (http://www.oakland.edu/GCC)

The university offers students personal counseling, testing, psychotherapy, and consultations. The Counseling Center is located in the Graham Health Center (248-370-3465). In addition to counseling and psychotherapy, the Counseling Center can provide evaluations regarding learning problems and disabilities.

Free Services for Students (http://www.oakland.edu/free)

OU offers a number of free services to students, including free health, academic and career, financial, and recreation services.

APPENDIX F: EVENTS AND ACTIVITIES

The Writing Excellence Awards

Each year, the department invites submission of high quality student writing for the Writing Excellence Awards competition.

Projects are accepted in eight categories:

First-Year Writing Courses (WRT 102, 150, or 160)

- Category 1: Rhetorical Analysis
- Category 2: Analytical Essay
- Category 3: Research Essay

Upper-Level Writing or Writing-Intensive Courses

- Category 4: Research Project
- Category 5: Creative Nonfiction
- Category 6: Professional Writing

All Courses

- Category 7: Multi-Media Project
- Category 8: Reflective Project

Prizes will include $100 for first place, $75 for second place, and $50 for third place in each category. Students may submit their work in more than one category but only one paper per category. The judges will make only one award per student (or group) and reserve the right to allocate the awards in order to recognize the best writing in all categories. Additional information about the awards is available online at http://www.oakland.edu/wrt/excellence-awards.

The current competition covers the 2016 winter, spring, summer, and fall semesters. The deadline for submissions is January 15, 2017.

The Writing Marathon

During both the fall and winter semesters, the Department of Writing and Rhetoric hosts a Writing Marathon that is open to students and faculty from around the university. Participants meet at a central location, form small writing groups, and set off with paper, laptops, or tablets to spend a couple of hours roaming the campus, writing, and sharing their work with their group. When the marathon participants return from their travels around campus, some of the writers choose to read their work to the whole group. Some first-year writing students may receive extra credit in their classes for participating in the marathon.

APPENDIX G: EARN A WRITING AND RHETORIC MAJOR OR MINOR

The Writing and Rhetoric Major at Oakland University was awarded a 2016 Writing Program Certificate of Excellence from the Conference on College Composition and Communication (CCCC), the national organization for collegiate writing programs. Established in 2004, this award honors a small number of writing programs annually for their focus on curricular excellence, student engagement, and overall program quality.

A Bachelor of Arts in writing and rhetoric prepares students for work as writers, editors, digital media composers, and educators in a variety of public, private, and educational settings. The writing and rhetoric major offers students focused tracks in professional writing, writing for digital media, and writing studies to prepare them to write, compose, and edit in a variety of professional contexts.

To earn a Bachelor of Arts in writing and rhetoric, students complete a minimum of 40 credits in writing and rhetoric coursework, including three required courses:

- WRT 340 Contemporary Issues in Writing and Rhetoric
- WRT 342 History of Rhetoric
- WRT 394 Literacy, Technology, and Civic Engagement

Our majors also complete four courses (16 credits) in one of the three tracks listed below:

1. Professional Writing

WRT 331: Introduction to Professional Writing (required)
Plus 3 courses from the following:

- o WRT 305: Advanced Writing
- o WRT 333: Editing
- o WRT 335: Human Services
- o WRT 381: Science Writing
- o WRT 382: Business Writing
- o WRT 386: Creative Nonfiction
- o WRT 486: Advanced Creative Nonfiction

2. Writing for Digital Media

WRT 232: Introduction to Writing for Digital Media (required)
Plus 3 courses from the following:

- o WRT 231: Podcasting
- o WRT 233: Digital Storytelling
- o WRT 330: Digital Culture
- o WRT 332: Rhetoric of Web Design
- o WRT 334: Rhetoric and Video Games

3. Writing Studies

WRT 329: Introduction to Writing Studies (required)
Plus 3 courses from the following:

- o WRT 320: Writing Center Studies and Tutoring Practice
- o WRT 350: Service Learning
- o WRT 360: Global Rhetorics
- o WRT 364: Writing about Culture
- o WRT 414: Teaching Writing

All majors will also complete two additional elective courses (8 credits) in writing and rhetoric. For their capstone experience, students must complete WRT 491: Capstone (Internship or Senior Thesis).

To earn a minor in writing and rhetoric, students must complete a minimum of 20 credits at the 200 level or above.

Department of Writing and Rhetoric

1. Core courses — 8 credits

   a. one course from the following:

   - WRT 232 - Introduction to Writing for Digital Media
   - WRT 329 - Introduction to Writing Studies
   - WRT 331 - Introduction to Professional Writing

   b. one course from the following:

   - WRT 340 - Contemporary Issues in Writing and Rhetoric
   - WRT 342 - History of Rhetoric
   - WRT 394 - Literacy, Technology, and Civic Engagement

2. 12 credits from additional WRT courses at the 200 level or above.

For more information, visit the Department of Writing and Rhetoric website: http://wwwp.oakland.edu/wrt/BA/ or contact Jim Nugent, Director of the Major, nugent@oakland.edu